The Complete Baking Cookbook For Young Chefs

Table of Contents

INTRODUCTION 1

CHAPTER 1: REASONS WHY YOU SHOULD LEARN HOW TO BAKE 2

CHAPTER 2: BREAKFAST RECIPES 5
- Cinnamon Raisin Swirl Bread 5
- Baked Eggs and Spinach in Sweet Potato Boats 5
- Breakfast Toast Cups 6
- Breakfast Baked Potatoes 7
- Super Easy Banana Muffins 7
- Baked Oatmeal Donuts 8
- Savory Keto Breakfast Cookies 9
- Cheesy Baked Eggs 9
- Eggs Baked in Avocado 10
- Lemon Poppy Seed Baked Oatmeal 10
- Mixed Berry Vanilla Baked Oatmeal 11
- Egg-cellent muffin cups 12
- The Ultimate Waffles 12
- Peach Melba Breakfast Pops 13
- Simple scrambled eggs 14
- Whole-Grain Blueberry Muffins 14

CHAPTER 3: MAIN DISHES RECIPES 16
- Pasta with homemade tomato sauce 16
- Spaghetti Bolognese 17
- Spaghetti Marinara 17
- Rigatoni Bolognese 18
- Goblin green pasta 19
- Fettuccine Alfredo 19
- Herby pesto pasta 20
- Beef and Mushroom Burgers 21
- Butterfly quesadillas 21
- Butternut mac 'n' cheese 22
- Easy peasy mac and cheesy 23
- Black Bean Burgers 24
- Tomato Spaghetti 25
- Vegetable Wraps 26
- Sweet Potato and Black Bean Quesadilla 27
- Vegetable Soup 27

Tomato Soup	28
Lima Bean Stew	29
Mushroom Sliders	30
Fish Tacos	30
Shrimp Fried Rice	31
Meatloaf	32
Sloppy Joes	33
Honey-roasted carrots with rosemary	34
Summery corn and watermelon salad	34
Balsamic-glazed carrots	35
Panzanella salad	35
Roasted baby fennel gratin	36
Kale chips	36
Minty avocado-melon mix	37
Shaved fennel salad	38
Grainy mustard-potato salad	38
Broccoli rabe puree	38
Turkey & Cucumber Salad Wraps	39
Nutty parmesan-kale salad	39
Brussels sprout stir-fry	40
Sauteed broccolini	40
Egg salad and toast points	41
Cucumber and tomato salad	41
Roasted cauliflower with dipping sauce	42
Green papaya and bell pepper salad	42
Roasted brussels sprouts and shallots	43
Summer strawberry salad	43

CHAPTER 4: COOKIES RECIPES 45

Honey Cookies	45
Spiced Oatmeal Cookies	45
Double Butterscotch Cookies	46
Jelly Bean Cookies	46
Classic Peanut Butter Cookies	47
Blueberry Bars	48
Superseded Slice	48
Garlic Dough Balls	49
Homemade Dry Pebble Cookies	49
Mushroom Cookies	50
Madeleine Cookies	50
"Peach" Cookies	51
Flour Cookies	51

    Snowball Christmas Cookies 52
    Coffee Gingersnap Cookies 53
    Peanut Butter Nutella Cookies 53
    Honey Lemon Cookies 54
    Butter Vanilla Cookies 54
    Fudgy Chocolate Cookies 55

CHAPTER 5: CAKES RECIPES 56
    Carrot cakes with Orange and Honey Syrup 56
    Little pistachio cakes 56
    Cauliflower cheesecake 57
    Lemon Drizzle cake 58
    Orange cake 58
    Rainbow Cake in a Jar 59

CHAPTER 6: PIES RECIPES 60
    Cherry Pie 60
    Lemon Whipped Cream Pie 60
    Blueberry Pie 61
    Oreo Butterscotch Pie 62
    Strawberry Pie 62
    Apple Pie 63

CHAPTER 7: SNACKS AND DESSERTS RECIPES 64
    Cheddar Biscuits 64
    Lemon Raspberry Muffins 64
    Blueberry Pound Cake 65
    Pizza Pockets 65
    Croissants 66
    Almond-Raisin Granola 67
    Jam Pockets 67
    Banana Bread 68
    Cranberry Ice-Cream Pie 68
    Cookie Dough Bites 69
    Surprise Pie 69
    Easy Fudge 70
    Apple Cake 70
    Key Lime Pie 71
    Lemon Squares 71
    Honey Pear Crisp 72
    Frozen Fruit Bites 72
    Honey Milk Balls 73
    Banana Bread Cobbler 73

Yummy Chocolate Cake 74
Walnut-coconut Coffee Cake 75
Raspberry Supreme Cheesecake 75
White Chocolate Torte 76
Raspberry Swirl Cheesecake Pie 77
Cherry Cheese Delight 77
Zucchini Chip Cupcakes 78
Cinnamon Cupcakes 78

CHAPTER 8: FROSTING RECIPES 80
Vanilla Buttercream Frosting 80
Hot Chocolate Whipped Cream Cake 80
Cream Cheese Frosting 81
Chocolate Frosting 82
Peanut Butter Frosting 82
Vanilla Cloud Frosting 82
Lemon frosting 83
Chocolate Glaze 83

CONVERSION CHART 84
CONCLUSION 87

Introduction

Many parents don't know how to interact with their kids. They don't know how to make them learn important skills and utilize their creativity and curiosity. It's fine if you're one of those parents. Whether one is a new or old parent, everyone encounters difficulty in raising their kids. You gradually learn the best ways to handle your children, and this comes with many years of experience. The important thing is that you are looking to find solutions and want to do the best for your child.

Even though you are well intended, children of all ages try to resist your teachings and run away from work. Whether your child is six or sixteen, they will always find excuses not to learn to cook. Fast food joints can hold the blame, but they are not the only problem. The home dishes we make look complex; many take hours to make and require a particular set of skills. You need to make cooking fun for them so they, happily, join you in your kitchen. They will grow up without fearing Ingredients and never live on just pasta and bread when they are on their own. They will gain confidence and increase their ability to connect with others.

If you want the best for your kids, you need to introduce them in the kitchen as soon as their motor skills activate. You'll be surprised by what little kids can do! If you give them the opportunity, they will not only live up to your expectations, but they will exceed them.

Now, you might wonder, "Where can I find healthy recipes that my kids can easily make?" No need to look any further. This book has all the knowledge that your child needs to start their steps in the kitchen.

Nowadays, you will see that many products targeted at children are usually sugary treats and chips. Children are not generally good at understanding the harmful effects of these threats, and they usually make them feel fat and sluggish. We can't blame them for making the wrong choice, but we can tell them what healthy options are and show them that they can be as delicious as other products in the candy store.

Cooking involves skill-based tasks that everyone should learn. It teaches children how to read and follow instructions properly, as it enhances their ability to understand the material. All the measuring cups and teaspoons will make them accustomed to numbers and simple calculations. They will learn how to handle and use different veggies, fruits, and learn even more about Ingredients. It is a way to utilize their young energy to create something productive that will assist them later in life. They might grow up to become experts in the kitchen because you introduced them to it in such a fun and creative way. Most importantly, you will make great memories together, and your children will always remember and thank you for what you taught them.

So, now you know the benefits of cooking with your kids and teaching them the skills of the kitchen. Knowledge is useless if you don't apply it in your life. If your kid is more than 6 years old and can comfortably move around the house and play all day, then they are fine in the kitchen. With you by their side, they will start to learn to make these easy recipes, and in time, will begin to prepare them without you around. It will become a massive time saver. Don't sleep on this great idea. If you don't take action now, you might miss this amazing opportunity to help your kids. Start cooking with them today and reap the benefits.

Chapter 1:

Reasons why you should learn how to bake

Baking is a great creative outlet and a great way to let off steam.

If you're learning how to bake, you will find that working with the dough and pounding it out is a great way to let off the steam of a long school day or a long week. Stressed out thinking about report cards or that exam? Try beating up some pizza dough until you can make something amazingly delicious out of it!

Learning how to bake expands your mind and helps you to understand more about the flavors and customs of the world around you.

Baking new and wonderful things from all around the world can show you a lot about the flavors and customs that come from all over the world. Learning about new cultures and their customs helps us to be more connected as a human race, and allows us to be more open to other new experiences in the future.

Baking your delicious items can save you lots of money while keeping your home stocked with some of the most delicious foods that you'll love to have time and time again!

Buying brownies, for instance, at the bakery can cost as much as $15 for a nice, big batch! When you make your brownies at home, whether from a mix or scratch, you will be saving an average of about a dollar per brownie! With savings like that, it's a wonder anyone ever lets professionals do their baking for them, right? Well, if you get nice and experienced at making baked goods, you can be the person that all your friends and family call when they're looking for the most delicious baked goods that anyone can make!

Baking with the people that we know and love can be such a wonderful bonding experience. Learning together, rolling up your sleeves, talking about the recipe, getting to know more about how baking works and how each of the Ingredients interacts with one another, and working together to make something truly delicious is a wonderful way to spend time with someone that you care about. Consider finding a recipe that you and friends can follow the next time they come over to visit, once you've gained a little bit of baking skill. Consider having an adult help you to roll out your dough to make biscuits or croissants for the morning after an awesome sleepover with your pals!

Expressing yourself through baking is a wonderful way to go.

When you start to learn more about baking, and you start to remember how to make certain things, you will find that you can express yourself and make your wonderful creations in the kitchen. What an excellent feeling!

Cooking is a fun and exciting journey. You mix, play, and in the end, you have the treat to enjoy. However, this activity can turn into a disaster if you do not keep safety precautions in mind. It is especially important when children are involved. Safety should always be the first thing on your mind as a parent. There are many ways for you and your child to get injured if you are not careful about them.

The kitchen contains many objects that can be dangerous, and you need to be aware of environmental hazards as well. Some equipment and utensils have sharp edges, like knives, some equipment run on electricity like a toaster, and some equipment deal with heat and fire like the oven and stove. The kitchen is filled with leftovers and pieces of food that can promote the build-up of bacteria. Being aware of safety is a habit that you should develop in yourself, as well as in your children.

Instructions for kids

- Thoroughly read the entire recipe, so you know what you are doing

- Never use the stove and oven alone. Heat and flames can hurt you, so you have to be extra careful around them.

- Wash your hands before and after you are done with cooking. Use soap, and dry your hands after you clean.

- Put on an apron. Wipe your hands on the apron when they get dirty. If they are too dirty, then wash them.

- Clear and clean repeatedly. Don't make a mess in the kitchen. Throw something away immediately, and after you finish, clean the counter.

- Use the knife properly. It would be best if you use the proper technique when you use the knife.

- You choose a knife that is not too big in your hand. You should feel comfortable doing this.

- Grasp the handle tightly. Hold the cutting edge of the blade down. Place your index finger on the full side of the blade.

- Start cutting in constant motion with no distractions. Place the food lengthwise on the cutting board and push the blade away from you. Grip the food by your left hand, with your fingers tucked inwards.

Instructions for adults

- The most important thing in the kitchen is always to be aware of what you do. Pay full attention to the task at hand, and do not multitask. Doing so will minimize injuries in the kitchen. One little slip can lead to a very bad outcome.

- Always have all your equipment near you or fully prepared when you make a meal beforehand. Looking for something haphazardly while cooking the recipe may cause an accident.

- Before doing a step, like cutting, always plan on how to clean it. Always prepare a garbage bag or bin near your cutting board so that you can immediately throw away the skins and unwanted bits and pieces. If you are using a utensil, place the used ones separate from the other, and clean them immediately as well.

- Have important safety equipment near you, like gloves, oven mitts, paper towels, etcetera. You will always be prepared and never forget to use them when needed in a rush.

- Constantly wash your hands. You are using different Ingredients and touching all types of surfaces and equipment. The food needs to be as clean as possible and to ensure that, you must clean your hands often.

- Be aware of people in the kitchen. Do not bump into one another or accidentally hurt them. (Be extra aware of kids, as they like to move around a lot).

- Place knives and other sharp utensils, which should NOT be in reach of children, in a locked or high up drawer.

- Do not use metal or heatproof bowls for microwaving. They will also get very hot. Do not even use aluminum foil inside a microwave.

- Learn how to use a knife properly. Bad technique can lead to cuts and bleeding. Use a dull knife when children are around.

- Be careful about handling hot objects, especially hot liquids. Use gloves and never be in a rush.

- Don't wear anything loose, and this includes long loose sleeves, no dangling jewelry, no open long hair, etcetera. These are a fire hazard. Also, make sure to tie your and your child's hair to prevent it from going into food as well.

- When you use a pot, make sure the handles do not face yourself or your child. They should always face the opposite side. Also, keep potholders away from flames.

- If you spill something, clean it up immediately. Not only bacteria start to develop, but there can be more chances of you or your child slipping.

- Do not let food sit in the kitchen that may spoil. Meat and dairy can spoil quickly. They leave a bad smell along with attracting insects. Always put them in the refrigerator when you are not using them.

- Separate all the types of meat and store them in separate containers or boxes. Not doing so can lead to cross-contamination and food poisoning.

- Get a fire extinguisher and learn how to use it. Sometimes, flames get out of control, and you need to be fully prepared for such a situation.

Chapter 2:

Breakfast Recipes

Cinnamon Raisin Swirl Bread

Prep & cook time: 20 minutes

Serves 20

Ingredients

- 2 tbsp milk
- 1-1/2 cups water, warm
- 1 tbsp salt
- 2 tbsp shortening
- 3 tbsp white sugar
- 2 tbsp yeast, active dry
- 4 cups bread flour
- 1 cup raisins
- 2 tbsp brown sugar
- 2 tbsp softened butter
- 1 tbsp cinnamon, ground
- 1 tbsp melted butter

Directions

1. Place milk, water, salt, shortening, sugar, yeast, and flour in the bread machine pan. Use manufacturer's recommendation then select cycle and press start.
2. Add rising just 5 minutes before the kneading cycle is over if your bread machine has a fruit set.
3. Once the kneading cycle is over, remove the dough and place it on a surface that is lightly floured.
4. Roll your dough into a rectangle then spread with brown sugar, butter, and cinnamon. Divide into two equal parts.
5. Lightly grease two bread pans, 9x5inch, then place loaves in. cover and place in a warm place to rise for about 1 hour until double in size.
6. Meanwhile, preheat your oven to $350°F$.
7. Brush the loaves top with melted butter and place into the oven.
8. Bake for about 30-40 minutes until a brown crust and a hollow sound when tapped.
9. Enjoy.

Nutritional Information: Calories 59, Total fat 3.1g, Saturated fat: 1g, Total Carbs 8.3g, Net Carbs 8g, Protein 0.4g, Sugar 3g, Fiber 0.3g, Sodium 130mg, Potassium 39mg

Baked Eggs and Spinach in Sweet Potato Boats

Prep & cook time:1 hour 20 minutes

Serves 4

Ingredients

- 2 sweet potatoes, large
- Pepper and salt
- 1 tbsp butter
- 1 cup finely chopped baby spinach, packed
- 4 eggs

Directions

1. Preheat an oven to 400°F.
2. Bake sweet potatoes for about 45-60 minutes in the oven.
3. Halve each sweet potato and scoop most of its flesh out leaving a small flesh rim around the potato skin.
4. Season each half with pepper and salt.
5. Add butter cubes to each potato half then top with spinach. Season again with pepper and salt.
6. Break an egg carefully into each half.
7. Bake the potato halves in your preheated oven for about 15 minutes until the eggs cook to your liking.
8. Lastly, season once more with pepper and salt.
9. Serve and enjoy.

Nutritional Information: Calories 159, Total fat 7g, Saturated fat 3g, Total carbs 17g, Net carbs 14g, Protein 7g, Sugar 4g, Fiber 3g, Sodium 216mg, Potassium 111mg

Breakfast Toast Cups

Prep & cook time: 35 minutes

Serves 6

Ingredients

- 6 bread slices
- 2 tbsp butter
- Spinach, a large handful
- 1/4 cup cheese
- 6 eggs
- 6 cooked bacon slices
- Pepper and salt to taste

Directions

1. Preheat an oven to 375°F.
2. In the meantime, lightly spray 6 muffin tin cups with butter.
3. Roll out bread slices using a rolling pin making them rather thin.
4. Cut out circles, 4-5inch, from each bread slice corner. Preserve the bread scraps.
5. Half the circles and spray each with butter.
6. Place a small bread scrap into the bottom of each muffin tin. Make sure it covers ⅔ of the tin bottom.
7. Place 2 bread circles halves into each cup. Position them leaving minimal holes.
8. Divide and load the remaining Ingredients among the 6 muffin tins with egg going last.
9. Bake in your oven for about 15 minutes until egg whites are set and thoroughly white.
10. Remove from the oven and splash with pepper and salt.

11. Immediately serve and enjoy.

Nutritional Information: Calories 290, Total fat 20g, Saturated fat 7g, Total Carbs 14g, Net Carbs 13g, Protein 13g, Sugars 2g, Fiber 1g, Sodium 630mg, Potassium 170mg

Breakfast Baked Potatoes

Are you bored with the usual bread breakfast? These potatoes will give you a perfect breakfast switch. They are easy to make so perfect to keep a young Chef busy in the kitchen.

Prep & cook time: 1 hour 15 minutes

Serves 4

Ingredients

- 4 cleaned russet potatoes, large
- 1 tbsp black pepper
- 1 tbsp salt
- 1 cup cheddar cheese, shredded
- 4 large eggs
- 6 chopped crispy bacon strips
- 2 tbsp chives, chopped

Directions

1. Preheat your oven to 425°F.
2. Bake your potatoes for about 45-50 minutes until fork tender. Remove and let cool slightly. (Alternatively, microwave the potatoes for about 15-20 minutes until fork tender.)
3. Cut a round opening on each potato top and remove it. Scoop most of the center out using a spoon.
4. Place the boats on a baking sheet then splash each with pepper and salt.
5. Splash each with little cheese and crack an egg into each potato boat. Top with bacon then more cheese over the eggs.
6. Bake for about 10-15 minutes until egg whites are set but still runny yolks.
7. Remove and splash with chives.
8. Serve warm.

Nutritional Information: Calories 360, Total fat 14g, Saturated fat 7g, Total Carbs 39g, Net Carbs 37g, Protein 18g, Sugars 3g, Fiber 2g, Sodium 850mg, Potassium 990mg

Super Easy Banana Muffins

Looking for a crowd pleasure breakfast? Banana muffins are super easy to prepare, making them perfect for a large crowd.

Prep & cook time: 40 minutes

Serves 10

Ingredients

- 2 large bananas
- 1/2 cup of sugar, granulated
- 1/3 cup canola oil
- 1/2 tbsp vanilla extract
- 1/4 cup of sugar, light brown
- 1 eggs, large
- 1 tbsp cinnamon
- 1-1/2 cups all-purpose flour
- 1/2 tbsp baking soda

- 1/2 tbsp salt
- 1 tbsp baking powder

Directions

1. Preheat your oven to 425°F.
2. In a 12-cavity muffin pan, line 10 cavities with cupcake liners.
3. Place mashed bananas, granulated sugar, canola oil, vanilla, brown sugar, and egg in a mixing bowl, large, then vigorously whisk until combined and smooth.
4. Add cinnamon, flour, baking soda, salt, and baking powder to the mixing bowl and continue whisking until combined. Be careful to over-mix.
5. Divide equally the mixture among the cupcake liners then place the muffin pan in your oven.
6. Bake for about 5 minutes at 425°F.
7. Now reduce temperature to 350°F and continue to bake for about 14-16 minutes until a toothpick comes out clean when inserted.
8. Remove the muffin pan and let cool for about 5 minutes.
9. Serve and enjoy!

Nutritional Information: Calories 210, Total fat 8g, Saturated fat 1g, Total Carbs 30g, Net Carbs 29g, Protein 3g, Sugars 16g, Fiber 1g, Sodium: 250mg, Potassium 45mg

Baked Oatmeal Donuts

Baked oatmeal donuts are super easy for young Chefs to prepare. They are also packed with nutrients and are perfect for someone looking for a fun and healthy way to kick off the day

Prep time: 15 minutes, **Cook time:** 15 minutes; Serves 14

Ingredients

- 1/2 cup water
- 1/4 cup vanilla Greek yogurt
- 1/4 cup hemp hearts
- 1/4 cup pumpkin seeds
- 1/2 cup cranberries, dried
- 1-1/4 cups all-purpose flour
- 1 tbsp baking powder
- 1/2 tbsp salt
- 3/4 cup brown sugar
- 3/4 cup oats, old-fashioned
- 3 tbsp avocado oil
- 1 egg

Directions

1. Preheat your oven to 350°F.
2. Meanwhile, spray donut pans using cooking spray.
3. Combine water and Greek yogurt in a bowl. Set aside.
4. Combine all dry Ingredients in a large bowl.
5. Combine all wet Ingredients in a small bowl. Add water/yogurt mixture to this bowl
6. Pour the wet mixture into the dry mixture and stir to completely combine.

7. Scoop the batter equally into donut cavities. Fill each.
8. Bake for about 12-15 minutes until cooked through and done.
9. Remove and let cool slightly.
10. Now remove and transfer the donuts onto a cooling rack.
11. Serve and enjoy!

Nutritional Information: Calories 177, Total fat 5g, Saturated fat 2g, Total Carbs 27g, Net Carbs 26g, Protein 4g, Sugars 14g, Fiber 1g, Sodium 93mg, Potassium 147mg

Savory Keto Breakfast Cookies

This is a grain-free, keto breakfast cookie perfect for busy mornings since they can be prepared in advance. These cookies are delicious and are one of the easiest breakfast recipes for young Chefs that might become their favorite.

Prep & cook time: 25 minutes

Serves 12

Ingredients

- 3 eggs, large
- 1-1/2 cups almond flour
- 1 tbsp baking powder
- 1 cup finely shredded cheddar cheese
- Black pepper
- 1/2 tbsp salt

Optional:

- 3 cooked bacon strips, crumbled
- 1 minced scallion

Directions

1. Preheat your oven to 350°F. Use parchment paper to line a baking sheet.
2. Place eggs, almond flour, baking powder, cheese, black pepper, and salt in a mixing bowl. Mix using a rubber spatula until stiff and combined.
3. Fold in bacon and scallions if using.
4. Divide the mixture into mounds and place on the lined baking sheet, about 12 in a batch, and then smooth the edges into a circular shape with slightly dampened fingers.
5. Flatten the mound tops until cookies of ¾ inch thick.
6. Bake the cookies on the oven middle rack for about 14-16 minutes until the edges are lightly golden and firm.
7. When done, remove from the oven and let cool for about 5 minutes.
8. Serve and enjoy!

Nutritional Information: Calories 160, Total fat 14g, Saturated fat 4g, Total Carbs 4g, Net Carbs 2g, Protein 8g, Sugars 1g, Fiber 2g, Sodium 280mg, Potassium 55mg

Cheesy Baked Eggs

Looking for a great way to start your day? These cheesy baked eggs are very easy to make and can be customized to your liking.

Prep time: 20 minutes

Serves 1

Ingredients

- 1 tbsp softened butter
- 2 tbsp milk, half and half or cream
- 2 large eggs
- Pinch of black pepper
- Pinch of salt
- 2 tbsp cheddar cheese, shredded
- 1 tbsp parmesan cheese, grated

Directions

1. Preheat your oven to 400°F.
2. In the meantime, coat inside of an oven ramekin, 8-ounces, with butter.
3. Whisk milk and eggs in a bowl, small.
4. Stir in pepper, salt, and cheeses.
5. Pour the batter into the ramekin.
6. Bake for about 15-18 minutes until eggs are cooked through.
7. Let cool for about 5 minutes and serve.
8. Enjoy!

Nutritional Information: Calories 358, Total fat 28g, Saturated fat 14g, Total Carbs 2g, Net Carbs 1g, Protein 22g, Sugars 1g, Fiber 1g, Sodium 450mg, Potassium 177mg

Eggs Baked in Avocado

Are you a young Chef looking for healthy and fun breakfast ideas? This egg baked in avocado is amazing. It's quick and easy to make. Trust me you will enjoy it.

Prep time: 25 minutes

Serves 4

Ingredients

- 2 extra-large avocados
- Black pepper
- Salt
- 4 eggs

Directions

1. Preheat your oven to 400°F.
2. Half the avocados and discard the pits. Now scoop out avocado flesh from each half. Leave 1/2-inch flesh border in the skin then reserve scooped out flesh.
3. Arrange the halves in a baking dish, square, with the cut side up.
4. Splash cavities with pepper and salt then crack an egg carefully into each half.
5. Season with pepper and salt to taste.
6. Bake for about 15-20 minutes on the oven middle rack until egg whites are set.
7. Make sure eggs are done then remove from the oven.
8. Serve immediately.

Nutritional Information: Calories 240, Total fat 20g, Saturated fat 3.5g, Total Carbs 11g, Net Carbs 3g, Protein 9g, Sugars 2g, Fiber 8g, Sodium 270mg, Potassium 590mg

Lemon Poppy Seed Baked Oatmeal

This is a healthy breakfast that is comforting, creamy, and lightly sweet. Lemon poppy seed baked oatmeal is pretty fabulous and I think everyone is going to love it.

Prep & cook time: 35 minutes

Serves 8

Ingredients

- 3 cups rolled oats, old-fashioned
- 3 eggs, large
- 2 cups vanilla almond milk, unsweetened
- 1/4 cup honey
- 1/4 tbsp Meyer lemon juice, fresh
- 1 tbsp Meyer lemon zest
- 1 tbsp vanilla extract, pure
- 1/4 tbsp salt
- 1 tbsp baking powder
- 1 tbsp poppy seeds

Directions

1. Preheat your oven to 350oF then lightly grease baking, medium. Set aside.
2. Mix all the Ingredients in a bowl, medium, until well combined.
3. Transfer into the baking dish.
4. Bake for 20-25 minutes in the oven while uncovered.
5. Enjoy!

Nutritional Information: Calories 204, Total fat 2.9g, Saturated fat 1g, Total Carbs 34g, Net Carbs 27.6g, Protein 3.5g, Sugars 12g, Fiber 6.6g, Sodium 240mg, Potassium 179mg

Mixed Berry Vanilla Baked Oatmeal

This is a perfect breakfast meal for a busy morning. Bake in advance and reheat needed portions. This oatmeal is filled with fresh berries, maple syrup, oats, and fragrant vanilla.

Prep & cook time: 50 minutes

Serves 6-8

Ingredients

- 3 cups rolled oats, old-fashioned
- 1 tbsp salt
- 1-1/2 tbsp baking powder
- 3 cups fresh berries
- 2 lightly beaten eggs
- 2 tbsp pure vanilla extract
- 1/2 cup pure maple syrup
- 2-1/2 cups vanilla almond milk, unsweetened
- 3 tbsp butter, unsalted

Directions

1. Preheat your oven to 350oF.
2. Grease a 3-quart baking dish and set aside.
3. Combine oats, salt, and baking powder in a bowl then place half of the mixture into the baking dish.
4. Top with half of the berries then add the remaining mixture.

5. Whisk eggs, vanilla, maple syrup, almond milk, and butter in a mixing bowl then pour over oats.

6. Top with remaining berries then shakes your baking dish forth and back, from side to side. This is to allow the wet mixture to move down to the oats.

7. Bake for about 25-40 minutes uncovered until mixture is set and oats are tender.

8. Serve immediately with a milk splash. (alternatively, cool, cover, and then refrigerate to reheat later)

Nutritional Information: Calories 267, Total fat 8g, Saturated fat 3g, Total Carbs 42g, Net Carbs 38g, Protein 6g, Sugars 17g, Fiber 4g, Sodium 304mg, Potassium 277mg

Egg-cellent muffin cups

Prep & cook time: 50 minutes

Serves: 12

Ingredients

- Olive oil or butter, for greasing the muffin tin
- 1 Roma tomato
- 1 bell pepper
- 6 ounces thick-cut deli ham (optional, leave out if vegetarian)
- 2 cups baby spinach
- ⅛ cup red onion
- 12 eggs
- ½ cup shredded Cheddar cheese (or any cheese)
- ½ cup milk
- ½ teaspoon salt
- Pepper, to taste

Directions

1. *Oil the muffin tin, and preheat the oven.* Use your fingers or a paper towel to spread olive oil or butter all over the inside of the muffin tin cups. Preheat the oven to 350°F.

2. *Cut the veggies and ham.* Using a cutting board and a kid-safe knife, cut the tomato into 4 pieces. Then cut the 4 large pieces into small cubes. Cut the bell pepper in half. Take the seeds out of the bell pepper. Cut the bell pepper into small cubes. If using ham, cut it into small, bite-size pieces. Chop up the baby spinach. Using a sharp knife, peel and mince the red onion.

3. *Beat the eggs, and stir the wet Ingredients.* In a medium bowl, crack 1 egg. Remove any shells, and pour the egg into a large bowl. Repeat with the next 11 eggs. Beat the eggs with a whisk until combined. Add the cheese, milk, salt, and pepper. Using a wooden spoon, stir until smooth. Mix the tomato, bell pepper, ham (if using), spinach, and onion into the egg mixture. With a ladle, scoop the mixture into the muffin tins, filling them three-quarters full.

4. *Bake the muffins.* Bake in the oven for 25 to 30 minutes, until the eggs look solid and puff up. Let the muffins cool for a few minutes, then run a butter knife around the edge of each muffin to help lift it out of the tin. Serve warm.

The Ultimate Waffles

Prep & cook time: 30 minutes

Serves: 8

Ingredients

- ½ cup old-fashioned oats, uncooked
- 1½ cups low-fat buttermilk
- 1 cup whole wheat flour
- 1 cup pecans, chopped
- 2 teaspoons baking powder
- ½ teaspoon baking soda
- ½ teaspoon cinnamon
- ½ teaspoon salt
- 2 large eggs
- 3 tablespoons vegetable oil
- 2 tablespoons honey
- 1 tablespoon vanilla extract
- 2 cups strawberries
- butter and honey for serving, optional

Directions

1. *Preparing the Ingredients.* Preheat oven to 225°F. In a medium bowl, combine oats and buttermilk. Let soak for 20 minutes. Preheat the waffle maker. In a large bowl with a wire whisk, mix flour, pecans, baking powder, baking soda, cinnamon, and salt. In a medium bowl, whisk eggs, oil, honey, and vanilla until blended. Add egg mixture and oat mixture to flour mixture. Stir until just combined (small lumps are okay).

2. *Cook.* Spray waffle maker with nonstick cooking spray. Pour ⅓ cup batter onto heated waffle maker. Close waffle maker; cook for 3 minutes or until deep golden brown. Place waffle directly on the oven rack to keep warm. Repeat with the remaining batter.

3. Serve with strawberries, butter, and more honey, if using.

Peach Melba Breakfast Pops

Prep & cook time: 10 minutes plus 8 hours freezing time

Serves: 6

Ingredients

- ⅔ cup vanilla Greek yogurt
- 2 tablespoons honey
- 2 small ripe peaches, chopped (about 1½ cups)
- ¼ cup raspberries halved
- ½ cup granola

Directions

1. *Preparing the Ingredients.* In a blender, combine yogurt, honey, and three-fourths of peaches until the mixture is smooth. Distribute raspberries and remaining peaches among 6 to 8 ice pop molds.

2. Fill each mold with about ¼ cup yogurt mixture, tapping to distribute, leaving ½ inch unfilled. Top with granola; pack granola tightly into yogurt until yogurt reaches the top of the mold.

3. Freeze for 6 to 8 hours or until solid.

Nutritional Per Serving: Calories: About 95, Protein: 3G, Carbohydrates: 30G, Total Fat: Saturated Fat: 1G), Fiber: 2G, Sodium: 30M

Simple scrambled eggs

Prep & cook time: 15 minutes

Serves: 4

Ingredients

- 6 to 8 eggs
- Kosher salt
- Freshly ground black pepper
- 4 tablespoons butter
- Flake salt, such as Maldon, for finishing
- delicious additions
- Sautéed broccoli or mushrooms
- Shredded cheese, folded in or finely shredded to top
- Minced scallions or chives
- Diced tomatoes
- Bacon or ham

Directions

1. *Beat the eggs.* Crack the eggs into a small bowl, and whisk until frothy. Season with salt and pepper.
2. Add the eggs to the pan
3. Melt the butter in a medium sauté pan over medium heat, and then turn the heat to low as the butter foams. Pour the eggs in and let sit for a few seconds.
4. Cook the eggs
5. Use a spatula to nudge and stir the eggs, scraping the bottom continuously as you move them around the pan to help prevent sticking. Use the spatula to push the eggs from center-out, and then scrape the pan edge, swirling the outermost eggs into the center. Keep doing this until the eggs begin to look like pudding and then form into dense, rich egg curds, about 4 minutes.
6. Serve
7. Remove the pan from the heat while the eggs are still a little loose; they will continue to cook on the way from the pan to your plate. Sprinkle with a little flake salt and pepper, and eat at once.

Whole-Grain Blueberry Muffins

Prep & cook time: 40 minutes

Serves: 12

Ingredients

- 1 cup old-fashioned oats, uncooked
- 1 cup whole wheat flour
- ½ cup all-purpose flour
- ¼ cup plus 1 tablespoon packed brown
- sugar
- 2 teaspoons baking powder
- ½ teaspoon baking soda
- ½ teaspoon salt
- 1 cup low-fat buttermilk
- ¼ cup of orange juice
- 2 tablespoons vegetable oil
- 1 large egg
- 1 teaspoon vanilla extract

- 2 cups blueberries

Directions

1. Preparing the Ingredients

2. Preheat oven to 400°F. Line 12-cup muffin pan with paper liners.

3. In a blender, place oats and blend until finely ground. In a large bowl with a wire whisk, mix oats, whole wheat flour, all-purpose flour, ¼ cup sugar, baking powder, baking soda, and salt. In a small bowl with a wire whisk, mix buttermilk, juice, oil, egg, and vanilla until blended. With a rubber spatula, fold egg mixture into flour mixture until combined; fold in blueberries.

4. Combine nuts and remaining 1 tablespoon sugar. Bake

5. Divide batter among prepared muffin cups; sprinkle with almond sugar. Bake for 22 minutes or until a toothpick inserted in the centers of muffins comes out clean. Cool in pan on a wire rack for 5 minutes. Remove muffins from pan; cool completely on wire rack.

Nutritional Per Muffin: Calories: About 170, Protein: 5G, Carbohydrates: 28G, Total Fat: 5G

(Saturated Fat: 1G), Fiber: 3G, Sodium: 270MG

Chapter 3:

Main Dishes Recipes

Pasta with homemade tomato sauce

Prep & cook time: 25 minutes

Serves: 4

Ingredients

- 8 tomatoes—heirloom varieties are ideal, with a few Roma tomatoes in the mix
- Ice water
- 2 tablespoons butter
- Olive oil, for drizzling
- 2 anchovies
- 2 garlic cloves, sliced thin
- Kosher salt
- 1 pound rigatoni or other ridged pasta
- Parmigiano-Reggiano, for serving
- Freshly ground black pepper

Directions

1. *Blanch tomatoes and peel the skins.* Set a medium saucepan filled with water to boil. Using a paring knife, cut an "X" shape into the bottom of each tomato. Carefully lower 1 or 2 tomatoes into the water at a time and blanch for 1 minute. Use a slotted spoon to transfer the blanched tomatoes to a bowl filled with ice water. When cool enough to handle, peel the skins and discard, then cut larger tomatoes into chunks and smaller ones in half over a bowl to collect their juices. Repeat with the remaining tomatoes, and set aside.

2. *Make the sauce.* In the same saucepan over medium heat, melt the butter and a drizzle of olive oil together. When the butter foams, add the anchovies, letting them sizzle and melt into the buttery mix. Use tongs to break them apart as they dissolve. After a minute or two, add the garlic slices and stir to combine. When the garlic becomes fragrant, add the tomatoes.

3. *Stir the mixture together, and bring to a boil.* Once bubbling, lower the heat to a simmer so the mixture still bubbles, but less vigorously. Stir occasionally, simmering for 7 to 10 minutes, while you cook the pasta.

4. *Cook the pasta.* In a large pot, boil enough water to cook 1 pound of pasta, 2 to 3 quarts. Add 1 tablespoon kosher salt to the water once it reaches a rolling boil, just before adding the pasta. Cook the pasta according to package instructions, stirring immediately after adding it to the water so that the noodles don't stick together. Once the water returns to a boil, stir occasionally until al dente. Drain the pasta in a colander, reserving 1 cupful of the cooking liquid.

5. *Serve.* Add a spoonful or two of the cooking liquid to the sauce and stir to incorporate. Transfer the pasta into shallow bowls, and top with the chunky tomato sauce. Use a fine grater to shower the pasta with a little fresh Parm, followed by salt and pepper to taste. Leftover sauce can be refrigerated for up to 5 days or frozen for up to 2 months.

Spaghetti Bolognese

Prep: 45 minutes

Serves: 4

Ingredients

- 1 tablespoon olive oil
- 1 medium onion, chopped
- 3 garlic cloves, chopped
- ½ teaspoon salt
- 1 pound ground beef chuck
- 1 can (28 ounces) crushed tomatoes
- 2 tablespoons grated pecorino cheese
- ½ cup milk
- 1 pound spaghetti
- fresh basil leaves and grated pecorino cheese, optional

Directions

1. *Preparing the Ingredients.* In a large saucepot, heat oil over medium-high heat until hot. Add onion, garlic, and salt; cook for 10 minutes or until tender, stirring occasionally. Add beef. Cook, stirring and breaking up beef with a side of a spoon, for 5 minutes or until beef loses its pink color throughout. Add tomatoes; heat to boiling over high heat. Reduce heat and simmer for 10 minutes or until flavors are blended. Stir in pecorino and milk.

2. Meanwhile, cook pasta as the label directs. Drain.

3. Add pasta to the sauce, tossing to combine. Garnish with basil leaves and more pecorino, if using.

Nutritional Per Serving Calories: About 575, Protein: 27G, Carbohydrates: 21G, Total Fat: 21G

(Saturated Fat: 7G), Fiber: 6G Sodium: 485MG

Spaghetti Marinara

Prep: 30 minutes

Serves: 6

Ingredients

- Kosher salt
- 1 pound spaghetti
- 3 tablespoons extra-virgin olive oil
- 4 cloves garlic, thinly sliced
- 1 small onion, finely chopped
- 1 teaspoon dried oregano
- 1 28-ounce can whole peeled tomatoes
- ½ cup chopped fresh basil
- 2 tablespoons unsalted butter, cut into
- cubes

Directions

1. *Preparing the Ingredients.* Fill a large pot with water and season with salt. Bring to a boil over high heat. Add the spaghetti and cook as the label directs for al dente. Carefully remove 1 cup of the pasta cooking water with a liquid measuring cup; set aside. Carefully drain the spaghetti in a colander set in the sink.

2. Meanwhile, heat the olive oil in a large skillet over medium heat. Add the garlic and cook until golden around the edges, about 3 minutes. Add the onion, oregano, and 1 teaspoon salt. Cook, stirring with a wooden spoon until the onion is soft but not browned, about 10 minutes. Empty the tomatoes into a bowl and crush with your hands. Add to the skillet along with ½ cup water; continue cooking until the sauce is slightly reduced, about 20 minutes. Stir in the basil and season with salt. Keep warm over low heat.

3. *Finish and serve.* Add the spaghetti to the sauce along with the butter and ½ cup of the reserved cooking water. Increase the heat to medium and toss with tongs to coat, adding the remaining cooking water as needed to loosen the sauce. Use the tongs to serve the spaghetti.

Rigatoni Bolognese

Prep: 30 minutes

Serves: 4

Ingredients

- Kosher salt
- 12 ounces rigatoni
- 1 28-ounce can whole peeled tomatoes
- 4 cloves garlic (2 whole, 2 sliced)
- Freshly ground pepper
- 2 tablespoons extra-virgin olive oil
- 1 pound ground beef
- ¼ cup red wine or low-sodium beef or chicken broth

Directions

1. *Preparing the Ingredients.* Fill a large pot with water and season with salt. Bring to a boil over high heat. Add the rigatoni and cook as the label directs for al dente. Carefully remove ½ cup of the pasta cooking water with a liquid measuring cup; set aside. Carefully drain the rigatoni in a colander set in the sink.

2. Meanwhile, combine the tomatoes, 2 whole garlic cloves, and ½ teaspoon each salt and pepper in a food processor and puree; set aside.

3. Heat the olive oil in a large saucepan over medium-high heat. Add the remaining 2 sliced garlic cloves and cook, stirring with a wooden spoon, for 1 minute. Add the ground beef and cook, breaking up the meat with the wooden spoon, until browned, 5 minutes. Carefully pour out all but about 1 tablespoon of the drippings from the pan.

4. Add the wine or broth to the saucepan and cook until the pan is dry about 3 minutes. Add the tomato puree and stir with the wooden spoon to combine. Reduce the heat to medium and simmer, stirring occasionally, until thickened, 20 minutes; season with salt and pepper.

5. *Finish and serve.* Add the rigatoni to the pan and toss with the wooden spoon, adding the

reserved cooking water to loosen the sauce as needed. Spoon into bowls.

Goblin green pasta

Prep: 30 minutes

Serves: 8

Ingredients

- 2 teaspoons fresh oregano (optional)
- 1 teaspoon fresh thyme (optional)
- 4 cups fresh baby spinach
- ¼ cup slivered almonds
- ¼ cup fresh basil
- ¼ teaspoon black pepper
- 2 large garlic cloves
- 2 tablespoons vegetable broth or water
- 1 tablespoon olive oil
- 2 teaspoons freshly squeezed lemon juice
- 1¼ teaspoons salt, divided (will be added at two different times)
- ¼ cup shredded Parmesan cheese, divided
- 8 ounces uncooked whole-wheat farfalle (bowtie pasta)
- Diced tomatoes (optional)

Directions

1. *Make the pesto sauce.* If using the oregano and thyme, use a cutting board and a kid-safe knife to chop enough oregano to fill a teaspoon twice and enough thyme to fill it once. Put the spinach, almonds, basil, oregano and thyme (if using), pepper, and garlic in a food processor. Process until chopped. Add the broth, oil, lemon juice, and ¼ teaspoon of salt, and process until well blended. Carefully remove the blade. Spoon the sauce into a small bowl, and stir in half of the cheese.

2. *Cook the pasta.* Fill large pot three-quarters full with water, and place on the stove. Add the pasta and the remaining 1 teaspoon of salt, and bring to a boil over high heat. Cook according to package directions.

3. *Combine the pasta and sauce.* Drain the pasta in a colander, then toss with the pesto. Top with the diced tomatoes (if using) and the remaining cheese, and serve.

Fettuccine Alfredo

Prep: 30 minutes

Serves: 6

Ingredients

- Kosher salt
- 1 pound fettuccine
- 1½ cups heavy cream
- 6 tablespoons unsalted butter, cut into cubes
- ¼ teaspoon freshly grated nutmeg
- Freshly ground pepper
- 1 cup grated parmesan cheese, plus more for topping

Directions

1. *Preparing the Ingredients.* Fill a large pot with water and season with salt. Bring to a boil over high heat. Add the fettuccine and

cook as the label directs for al dente. Carefully remove ½ cup of the pasta cooking water with a liquid measuring cup; set aside. Carefully drain the fettuccine in a colander set in the sink.

2. Meanwhile, combine the heavy cream and butter in a large skillet. Bring to a simmer over medium-high heat, whisking to combine. Whisk in the nutmeg and ½ teaspoon each salt and pepper. Keep warm over low heat.

3. *Finish and Serve.* Add the fettuccine and cheese to the skillet. Increase the heat to medium and toss with tongs to coat, adding the reserved cooking water as needed to loosen the sauce. Use the tongs to serve the fettuccine and top with more parmesan.

Herby pesto pasta

Prep: 25 minutes

Serves: 4

Ingredients

- ⅓ cup nuts, such as pine nuts, walnuts, almonds, or pistachios
- 1 garlic clove
- ½ cup Parmigiano-Reggiano cheese, freshly shredded, plus extra for serving
- Olive oil, as needed
- 2 cups loosely packed fresh basil leaves
- ½ cup fresh parsley leaves
- 1 tablespoon kosher salt
- 1 teaspoon freshly squeezed lemon juice, to prevent oxidizing
- 1 pound fettuccine
- Flake sea salt, such as Maldon
- Freshly ground black pepper

Directions

1. Toast the nuts. Arrange nuts in a single layer on a toaster oven tray. Toast for 4 minutes, or until they become fragrant and their edges turn golden. You may agitate pan halfway through, circulating them for even toasting. Transfer nuts to a small dish to cool.

2. Make the pesto. Using a food processor, pulse the nuts, garlic, cheese, and enough olive oil to make a rough paste. Stop as needed to scrape down the sides of the bowl. Add the basil and parsley, a pinch of salt, and more olive oil, and pulse to combine. The mixture should resemble a bright green sauce. Drizzle the fresh lemon juice over the mixture once you are happy with the consistency.

3. Boil the pasta. In a large pot, boil enough water to cook 1 pound of fettuccine, about three quarts (12 cups). Add 1 tablespoon kosher salt to the water once it is at a rolling boil just before adding the pasta. Cook the pasta according to package instructions, stirring immediately after adding the pasta so that it doesn't stick together. Once the water returns to a boil, stir occasionally until al dente. Drain the pasta in a colander, and transfer to a large bowl, reserving 1 cupful of the cooking water for later.

4. Empty the pesto into the bowl of pasta. Use a rubber spatula to thoroughly scrape the bowl and underneath the blade, getting all the good bits out. Add a few spoons of the pasta water as you toss the noodles and pesto together. Use a large spoon in one

hand and the rubber spatula in the other to combine them well, coating the noodles in the sauce.

5. Serve. Twirl tangles of pasta into shallow bowls, spooning additional pesto on top as you like. Shower the pasta with a little more freshly grated cheese, season with salt and pepper, and enjoy at once. Leftover pasta will last up to 3 days, kept sealed in the refrigerator. If you saved any pesto separate from the pasta, transfer it to a jar and cover its surface directly with plastic wrap to slow oxidation, seal it, and keep refrigerated for up to 1 week.

Beef and Mushroom Burgers

Prep: 40 minutes

Serves: 4

Ingredients

- 8 ounces mushrooms
- 1 tablespoon Worcestershire sauce
- 12 ounces ground beef sirloin (90%)
- ¼ cup grated onion squeezed dry
- ¼ teaspoon ground black pepper
- 1 tablespoon vegetable oil
- 4 slices American cheese or cheddar cheese (about 3 ounces)
- 4 hamburger buns, split and toasted
- lettuce leaves and tomato slices

Directions

1. *Preparing the Ingredients.* In food processor with knife blade attached, pulse mushrooms and Worcestershire until mushrooms are finely chopped.

2. In a large bowl, combine mushroom mixture, beef, and onion until blended, but do not overmix. Shape meat mixture into 4 equal patties, each about 4 inches wide, handling meat as little as possible. Sprinkle pepper on both sides of the patties.

3. *Cook.* In 12-inch nonstick skillet, heat oil over medium heat until hot. Add patties. Cook for 5 minutes. Turn patties over; increase heat to medium-high. Top each patty with 1 slice of cheese. Cook for 4 minutes or until cheese melts.

4. Serve burgers on buns with lettuce and tomato.

Nutritional value Serving Calories: About 350, Protein: 27G, Carbohydrates: 28G, Total Fat: 14G Saturated Fat: 6G), Fiber: 2G, Sodium: 660MG

Butterfly quesadillas

Prep: 30 minutes

Serves: 1

Ingredients

- 1 teaspoon olive oil
- ½ small tomato
- ¼ red or yellow bell pepper
- Handful baby spinach
- 1 whole-wheat tortilla
- ¼ cup refried beans
- ¼ cup shredded cooked chicken (optional)
- ⅛ cup shredded Cheddar cheese

- 1 carrot stick
- 1 small grape tomato

Directions

1. Oil the pan, and cut the veggies

2. Use your fingers or a paper towel to spread the olive oil on the bottom of a large skillet or pan. Set the pan aside. On a cutting board, use a kid-safe knife to cut the tomato into small cubes. Cut 2 long slices of bell pepper, then cut the remaining bell pepper section into small cubes. Chop the baby spinach with the kid-safe knife or clean, kid-safe scissors.

3. *Assemble the quesadilla.* Lay the tortilla on a plate. With a butter knife, spread the refried beans on half of the tortilla, top the beans with the chopped veggies and cooked chicken (if using), and sprinkle the cheese on top of the veggies. Fold the tortilla in half.

4. *Heat the pan, and cook the quesadilla.* On the stovetop over medium heat, heat the oiled pan. Carefully place the folded quesadilla in the pan. Cook for 5 minutes on one side, until the cheese, has melted. Using a spatula, flip the quesadilla over, and let it cook for another 5 minutes, until slightly golden brown and crispy.

5. *Make the butterflies.* Take the quesadilla off the stove, and cut it in half. On a plate, put the two halves with the pointy sides facing each other; these are the wings. Place a carrot stick between the halves for the butterfly's body. Place the grape tomato at the top end of the carrot stick for the butterfly's head. Place the two bell pepper slices on top of the tomato to make the butterfly's antennas. Enjoy.

Butternut mac 'n' cheese

Prep: 1 hour 10 minutes

Serves: 4

Ingredients

- 4 tablespoons butter, divided, plus more for greasing ramekins
- 2 thick slices of rustic bread, crusts removed and torn into bite-size pieces
- ½ teaspoon kosher salt, plus a hefty pinch
- 12 ounces' macaroni
- ½ butternut squash, peeled, seeded, and sliced into inch-long bite-size pieces
- 2 cups of milk
- 3 tablespoons all-purpose flour
- ¼ teaspoon freshly grated nutmeg
- ¼ teaspoon freshly ground black pepper
- ¼ teaspoon cayenne pepper
- 1 ½ cups grated sharp white Cheddar cheese, divided
- 1 cup grated Gruyère cheese, divided

Directions

1. Prepare the ramekins, Butter 4 ramekins, and set aside on a baking sheet.

2. Toast the bread. Place the bread onto a toaster oven tray. In a small saucepan over medium heat, melt 1 tablespoon of butter, and drizzle the butter over the bread, stirring the pieces around the tray to coat. Toast the croutons until lightly crispy, about 5 minutes, and set aside.

3. Cook the pasta. *Set* a large pot filled with water over high heat, and bring to a rolling boil. Add 1 tablespoon salt, add the pasta, and stir well. Cook 3 minutes less than the package instructions say so that the pasta exterior is cooked and the inside is underdone. Transfer the pasta to a colander, and shake it a few times to drain well. Rinse the pasta briefly to stop it from cooking further and set aside.

4. Steam the squash. Fit a steamer basket inside a saucepan and add 1 inch of water. Cover and steam the squash pieces until slightly softened, 3 to 5 minutes. Use tongs to remove the squash from the basket, rinse under cold water, and set aside.

5. Preheat the oven to 375°F. Make the béchamel. In a small saucepan over medium-low heat, warm the milk. In the same pot, you used for cooking the pasta, over medium heat, melt the remaining 3 tablespoons of butter. When the butter foams, add the flour. Whisk the flour into the butter, stirring to fully combine. Continue whisking

6. Gradually pour in the hot milk. After pouring half in, whisk until the mixture has no lumps, then slowly add the remainder. Whisk constantly, until the mixture bubbles and becomes thick, 8 to 10 minutes. Combine the Ingredients for baking

7. Remove the pan from the heat, and stir in the salt, nutmeg, black pepper, cayenne pepper, 1 cup of Cheddar cheese, and ½ cup of Gruyère.

8. Add pasta and squash. Stir the cooked pasta and steamed squash into the cheesy béchamel sauce. Ladle the mixture into the ramekins. Sprinkle the remaining ½ cup of Cheddar cheese and ½ cup of Gruyère over the tops, then arrange the toasted croutons on top. Bake until the surfaces are golden, about 25 minutes.

9. Serve. Transfer the casseroles to a wire cooling rack, and allow to cool for 5 minutes. Serve the little mac-and-cheese ramekins warm on large plates.

Easy peasy mac and cheesy

Prep: 45 minutes

Serves: 8

Ingredients

- 8 ounces whole-wheat macaroni
- 1 teaspoon plus ¼ teaspoon salt, divided, plus more to taste
- 1 teaspoon olive oil
- 1 cup frozen peas
- 16 ounces pre-cut fresh broccoli florets (optional)
- 2 tablespoons butter
- ¼ cup flour
- 2 cups of milk
- 1 cup vegetable broth or chicken broth
- ⅛ teaspoon black pepper, plus more to taste
- 2 cups shredded Cheddar cheese
- ¼ cup shredded Parmesan cheese

Directions

1. Cook the pasta. Fill large pot three-quarters full with water. Add the macaroni and 1

teaspoon of salt. Heat the water on the stovetop over high heat until boiling. Cook, following package directions, then drain in a colander.

2. Cook the vegetables. Coat a large skillet or pan with 1 teaspoon of olive oil. Heat the pan on the stovetop over medium heat. Add the peas and broccoli (if using), and cook for about 10 minutes, stirring with a wooden spoon, until tender.

3. Make the cheese sauce. In the large pot over medium-low heat, melt the butter. Add the flour and, stirring constantly with a wooden spoon, cook for 2 minutes, or until the flour is pasty and golden. Turn the heat up to medium-high. Add the milk and broth, and whisk (Use a whisk or fork to stir Ingredients). Bring the mixture to a boil, whisking constantly. Continue cooking, whisking constantly, for about 5 minutes, or until the sauce becomes smooth and thick. Add the remaining ¼ teaspoon of salt and pepper. Turn off the stove. Add the Cheddar cheese, and mix until the cheese is melted.

4. Combine the mac and cheese. Add the macaroni and vegetables to the cheese sauce in the pot, and stir until combined. Stir in the Parmesan cheese. Serve hot.

Black Bean Burgers

Prep & cook time: 20 minutes

Serves: 3

Ingredients:

- 7.5 ounces canned black beans
- ¼ cup chopped white onion
- 2 2/3 tablespoons bread crumbs
- ¼ cup cornmeal
- 1 small egg, at room temperature
- 2 tablespoons olive oil

Extra Ingredients:

- 3 whole-wheat hamburger buns
- 3 leaves of lettuce
- 3 slices of cheddar cheese

Directions:

Kid:

1. Peel the onion and chop it, crack the egg in a small bowl, and then whisk it lightly.

2. Drain the beans, place them in a medium bowl, and then mash with a fork until broken.

3. Add chopped onion, bread crumbs, and onion, and then stir until well combined.

Kid + **Adult:**

1. Divide the mixture into three portions and then shape each portion into a patty.

2. Place cornmeal in a shallow dish and then dredge each patty until coated.

3. Place a medium skillet pan over medium-high heat, add oil, and let it heat until warm.

4. Add the prepared patties into the pan and then cook them for 2 to 3 minutes per side until golden brown.

5. When done, transfer the patties to a plate lined with paper towels and let them rest for 5 minutes.

6. Meanwhile, cut each bun in half lengthwise, and then toast them until warm and golden brown.

Kid:

1. Assemble the burger and for this, take a bottom half of the burger bun, arrange a lettuce leaf on it, and then top with a fried black bean patty.

2. Place a cheese slice on the patty, cover with the top half of the bun, and then prepare the remaining two burgers in the same manner.

3. Serve burgers with salsa or ketchup.

Nutritional Information per Serving: Calories: *300 Cal;* Total Fat: *6 g;* Saturated Fat: *1 g;* Cholesterol: *35 mg;* Carbohydrates: *50 g;* Fiber: *7 g;* Sugar: *5 g;* Protein: *13 g;*

Tomato Spaghetti

Prep & cook time: 35 minutes
Yield: 4 plates

Ingredients:

- ½ bunch of basil, fresh
- 2 cans of whole peeled tomatoes, each about 14-ounce
- 1 medium white onion
- 1 teaspoon minced garlic
- 1 tablespoon olive oil
- 1 tablespoon balsamic vinegar
- 1 pound whole-wheat spaghetti, uncooked

Extra Ingredients:

- ½ ounce parmesan cheese
- ¾ teaspoon salt
- ¼ teaspoon ground black pepper

Directions:

Kid:

1. Pick the basil leaves, chop the stalks and three-fourth of the leaves and then reserve the remaining leaves for garnishing.

2. Peel the onion and then slice it, and then open the tomato can.

3. Grate the cheese and set it aside until required.

Adult:

1. Place a medium saucepan over medium heat, add oil and let it heat until warm.

2. Add sliced onion, stir until just mixed, and then cook for 7 minutes until golden and softened.

Kid + **Adult**:

1. Add basil stalks and garlic, stir until mixed, cook for 1 minute, and add canned tomatoes.

2. Break the tomatoes with the back of your spoon, stir in vinegar, salt, black pepper and then let the sauce cook for 3 minutes, covering the pan with its lid and stirring the sauce occasionally.

3. Then add chopped basil leaves, and continue cooking the sauce for 12 minutes.

4. **Adult**:

5. Meanwhile, place a large pot filled with 16 cups of water over medium-high heat, and bring it to a boil.

6. Then add spaghetti, cook it for 7 t0 8 minutes, or for the time stated on the package until it is al dente; this means spaghetti should be firm and soft enough to eat.

7. When spaghetti has cooked, reserve ¼ cup of the pasta liquid, drain the spaghetti into a colander and set aside until required.

Kid:

8. When 12 minutes are over, then switch the heat of tomato sauce to the low level, and then pour in enough pasta liquid until the sauce has turned semi-thick.

9. Continue cooking the sauce for 2 to 3 minutes or until beginning to bubble, add the cooked spaghetti, and then toss it well by using tongs until well coated.

10. Sprinkle basil leaves and cheese on top, divide spaghetti evenly among four plates, and then serve.

Nutritional Information per Serving: Calories: *271 Cal;* Total Fat: *4.7 g;* Saturated Fat: *0.7 g;* Cholesterol: *0 mg;* Carbohydrates: *49 g;* Fiber: *4.7 g;* Sugar: *5.9 g;* Protein: *9.4 g;*

Vegetable Wraps

Prep & cook time: 30 minutes

Yield: 2 wraps

Ingredients:

- 1 medium carrot
- 1 medium white onion
- 1 medium zucchini
- ½ cup sliced mushrooms
- ½ cup cream cheese
- 2 whole-wheat tortillas, about 8-inch

Extra Ingredients:

- ½ teaspoon salt
- ½ teaspoon ground black pepper
- 2 tablespoons olive oil

Directions:

Adult:

1. Switch on the oven, then set its temperature to 450 degrees F, and let it preheat.

Kid:

1. Peel the carrot, onion, and zucchini, and then cut the vegetables in ¼-inch thick slices lengthwise.

2. Transfer the carrot and onion in a medium bowl, add 1 tablespoon oil, ¼ teaspoon salt, and black pepper, and then toss until coated.

3. Spread the vegetables on a sheet pan, carefully place it into the preheated oven, and then let it bake for 10 minutes.

4. Meanwhile, place mushroom and zucchini into the bowl, add remaining oil, salt, and black pepper, and then toss until coated.

5. After 10 minutes of roasting, remove the sheet pan from the oven, add mushrooms and zucchini, then return the sheet pan into the oven, and continue roasting the vegetables for 10 minutes.

6. When vegetables have roasted, place tortillas in a clean working space, and then spread ¼ cup of cream cheese on top of each tortilla, leaving a 1-inch border.

7. Use a tong to divide roasted vegetables on the prepared tortillas.

8. Working on one tortilla at a time, fold it by folding its left and right side over vegetables, and then roll up the tortilla from the tortilla.

9. Roll up the other tortilla in the same manner, and then cut each wrap in half.

10. Serve immediately.

Nutritional Information per Serving: Calories: *498 Cal*; Total Fat: *29 g*; Saturated Fat: *10 g*; Cholesterol: *60 mg*; Carbohydrates: *48 g*; Fiber: *7 g*; Sugar: *7 g*; Protein: *10 g*;

Sweet Potato and Black Bean Quesadilla

Prep & cook time: 30 minutes

Yield: 2 quesadillas

Ingredients:

- 1 medium sweet potato
- ½ can black beans, about 14 ounces
- 2 tablespoons cilantro leaves
- ½ tablespoon taco seasoning
- 4 whole-wheat tortillas, about 8-inch
- ½ cup shredded cheddar cheese

Directions:

Kid:

1. Prick the sweet potato using a fork, place it in a microwave, and then cook for 5 minutes at a high heat setting.

2. After 5 minutes, remove sweet potato from the microwave, cool it for 5 minutes, and then cut the potato half lengthwise.

3. Scoop the flesh of sweet potato in a medium bowl, and then mash with a fork until smooth.

4. Add taco seasoning, cilantro, and black beans, and then stir until mixed.

Adult:

1. Place a large skillet pan over medium heat, and let it heat until hot.

Kid:

1. Place a tortilla in a clean working space, spread half of the sweet potato mixture on top, sprinkle with ¼ cup of cheese, and then top with the second tortilla.

Adult:

1. Carefully place the prepared quesadilla into the hot pan, cook it for 4 minutes until the cheese melts, then flip the quesadilla, and continue cooking for 2 minutes.

2. Transfer cooked quesadilla to a plate, prepare another quesadilla using remaining tortillas, sweet potato mixture, and cheese and then cook it.

3. Serve straight away.

Nutritional Information per Serving: Calories: *293 Cal*; Total Fat: *9 g*; Saturated Fat: *3.6 g*; Cholesterol: *20 mg*; Carbohydrates: *35 g*; Fiber: *10 g*; Sugar: *2 g*; Protein: *17 g*;

Vegetable Soup

Prep & cook time: 50 minutes

Yield: 4 bowls

Ingredients:

- ½ of a medium head of cauliflower
- 4 medium carrots
- 1 medium white onion, peeled, diced
- 1 large tomato, diced
- 1 ½ cup kale, fresh
- 1 teaspoon minced garlic
- 4 cups vegetable broth

Extra Ingredients:

- 1 teaspoon salt
- ½ teaspoon ground black pepper
- 1 tablespoon olive oil

Directions:

Adult:

1. Peel the onion and carrot, and then dice the vegetables and tomato.

Kid:

1. Tear the leaves of kale, and then tear the cauliflower florets.

Adult:

1. Place a large pot over medium heat, add oil, and let it heat until hot.

Adult + *Kid*:

1. Add onion and garlic, stir in 1/8 teaspoon salt, and cook the vegetables for 4 minutes.
2. Add carrots, stir in 1/8 teaspoon salt, and then continue cooking for 4 minutes.
3. Add cauliflower florets, stir in ½ teaspoon salt and continue cooking for 3 minutes.

Kid:

1. Add kale leaves, add 1/8 teaspoon salt, stir until mixed, and then cook the vegetables for 4 minutes.

Adult + *Kid*:

1. Pour in the vegetable broth, stir in remaining salt and black pepper, switch heat to a high level, and boil the soup for 3 minutes, covering the pot with its lid.
2. Switch heat to the low level, simmer the soup for 20 minutes, and then stir in tomatoes.
3. Continue cooking the soup for 2 minutes, remove the pot from heat, stir the soup and then ladle it evenly among four bowls.
4. Serve straight away.

Nutritional Information per Serving: *Calories:* 167 Cal; *Total Fat:* 7 g; *Saturated Fat:* 1 g; *Cholesterol:* 0 mg; *Carbohydrates:* 23 g; *Fiber:* 6 g; *Sugar:* 11 g; *Protein:* 4 g;

Tomato Soup

Prep & cook time: 55 minutes

Yield: 4 bowls

Ingredients:

- 1 medium white onion, diced
- 2 cans of diced tomatoes with liquid, each about 14.5 ounce
- 1 teaspoon minced garlic
- ¼ teaspoon dried thyme
- 2 tablespoons flour
- 1 ½ tablespoon olive oil

- 2 cups vegetable broth

Extra Ingredients:

- ¾ teaspoon sea salt
- ¼ teaspoon ground black pepper

Directions:

Adult:

1. Place a large pot over medium heat, add oil and let it heat.

Adult + *Kid*:

1. Add onion and garlic into the pot and then cook for 9 minutes until the onion turns soft.
2. Stir in the flour, add tomatoes and thyme, pour in the broth, and then stir until combined.

Kid:

1. Add salt and black pepper and stir until combined.

Adult + *Kid*:

1. Cover the pot with its lid and then simmer the soup for 40 minutes until cooked.
2. Remove the pot from the heat, let it cool for 5 minutes, and then puree it by using an immersion blender for 1 to 2 minutes until smooth yet lumpy.
3. If an immersion blender is not available, blend the soup in a food processor, one-fourth of its portion at a time, and then return it into the pot.
4. Place the pot over medium heat, and then cook it for 2 minutes until hot.
5. Ladle the soup among four bowls and then serve.

Nutritional Information per Serving: *Calories:* 130 Cal; *Total Fat:* 5 g; *Saturated Fat:* 1 g; *Cholesterol:* 0 mg; *Carbohydrates:* 18 g; *Fiber:* 7 g; *Sugar:* 7 g; *Protein:* 2 g;

Lima Bean Stew

Prep & cook time: 20 minutes

Yield: 5 bowls

Ingredients:

- 2 jars of lima beans, each about 12 ounces
- 1 medium white onion, peeled, diced
- 2 teaspoons minced garlic
- 2 tablespoons red chili paste
- 1 tablespoon olive oil
- 1 cup of water
- 1 cup tomato sauce

Extra Ingredients:

- 1 teaspoon salt
- ½ teaspoon ground black pepper

Directions:

Adult:

1. Place a large saucepan over medium heat, add oil and when hot, add onion and garlic and then cook for 5 minutes or until softened.

Adult + Kid:

1. Stir in red chili paste, cook for 1 minute, add beans and tomato sauce, and then pour in water.

2. Stir until combined, switch heat to the low level, and then cook the stew for 5 minutes or more until hot.
3. Season the stew with salt and black pepper, ladle it evenly among five bowls, and then serve.

Nutritional Information per Serving: Calories: *174 Cal;* Total Fat: *3 g;* Saturated Fat: *0 g;* Cholesterol: *0 mg;* Carbohydrates: *31 g;* Fiber: *7 g;* Sugar: *4 g;* Protein: *9 g;*

Mushroom Sliders

Prep & cook time: 45 minutes

Yield: 4 sliders

Ingredients:

- 2 portabella mushrooms
- 8 slices of red onion
- 8 slices of tomato
- 8 small whole-grain dinner rolls
- ¼ cup balsamic vinaigrette

Extra Ingredients:

- ½ teaspoon salt
- 1/3 teaspoon ground black pepper

Directions:

Kid:

1. Remove the stem from each mushroom, then place mushrooms in a plastic bag, and then add the vinaigrette.
2. Seal the bag, turn it upside down until mushrooms have coated with the vinaigrette, and then let them marinate for 30 minutes at room temperature.

Adult:

1. Meanwhile, slice the tomato and onion, and set aside until required.
2. After 30 minutes, remove mushrooms from the plastic bag, drain them, and then season both sides with black pepper and salt.

Adult:

1. Place a grill pan over medium heat, spray it with oil, and let it heat until hot.
2. Place the seasoned mushrooms on the grill, gill-side down, and then cook for 4 minutes per side until thoroughly cooked and developed grill marks.
3. When done, transfer grilled mushrooms to a plate lined with paper towels, and then cut each mushroom into the quarter.

Kid:

1. Assemble the slider and for this, cut the dinner in half, and then place quarter pieces of one mushroom on the bottom half of a dinner roll.
2. Top the mushroom with 4 slices of onion and tomato, and then cover with the other half of the roll.
3. Prepare another slider in the same manner and then serve.

Nutritional Information per Serving: Calories: *165 Cal;* Total Fat: *4 g;* Saturated Fat: *1 g;* Cholesterol: *0 mg;* Carbohydrates: *29 g;* Fiber: *5 g;* Sugar: *8 g;* Protein: *5 g;*

Fish Tacos

Prep & cook time 20 minutes

Yield: 4 tacos

Ingredients:

- 4 taco shells
- 6 ounces white fish fillet
- ½ of a medium avocado
- ½ teaspoon dried basil
- 1 medium tomato
- 1 tablespoon olive oil
- 1 cup shredded lettuce

Extra Ingredients:

- ¼ teaspoon salt
- ¼ teaspoon ground black pepper
- ½ teaspoon ground cumin
- ½ tablespoon red chili powder

Directions:

Kid:

1. Take a shallow dish, place salt, black pepper, cumin, red chili powder, and basil in it, and then stir until combined.
2. Place fish fillet into the seasoning mix and then toss until coated evenly on all sides.

Adult:

1. Place a large skillet pan over medium heat, add oil and let it heat.

Adult + Kid:

1. Place the seasoned fish fillet in it and then cook it for 5 minutes per side until golden brown and cooked.

Kid:

1. When done, use a tong to transfer fish to a cutting board, let it rest for 2 minutes, and then shred it by using two forks.

Adult:

1. Read the baking instructions on the package of taco shells, and then bake them.
2. Chop the tomato and then chop the avocado.

Kid:

1. Assemble the taco and for this, evenly divide shredded fish among baked taco shells, add lettuce, avocado, and tomato and then serve.

Nutritional Information per Serving: Calories: *367 Cal;* Total Fat: *18 g;* Saturated Fat: *4 g;* Cholesterol: *51 mg;* Carbohydrates: *33 g;* Fiber: *6 g;* Sugar: *10 g;* Protein: *20 g;*

Shrimp Fried Rice

Prep & cook time: 30 minutes

Yield: 4 plates

Main Ingredients:

- ¾ cup frozen peas and carrots
- 8 ounces small shrimps, peeled, deveined
- 2 green onions, minced
- 4 cups cooked brown rice
- 1 tablespoon soy sauce
- 2 tablespoons olive oil
- 3 eggs, at room temperature

Extra Ingredients:

- ¼ teaspoon salt
- 1/8 teaspoon ground black pepper
- 1 teaspoon sesame oil

Directions:

Kid:

1. • Place shrimps in a medium bowl, add cornstarch, salt, and black pepper, stir until mixed, and then let them marinate at room temperature for 10 minutes.
2. • Crack eggs in a bowl and then beat them lightly.
3. • Place peas and carrots in a bowl and then defrost them in the microwave oven.

Adult:

1. Meanwhile, cook the rice according to the instruction on its package, and set aside until required.
2. Then place a large skillet pan over high heat, let it heat until hot, and then add 1 tablespoon oil.

Adult + Kid:

1. Add marinated shrimps to the pan, spread them in the pan so that the shrimps do not overlap, and then fry them for 30 seconds; do not stir.
2. Then flip the shrimps, continue frying them for another 30 seconds and transfer shrimps to a plate.

Adult:

1. Switch heat to medium level, add eggs, and then cook them for 3 to 4 minutes until scrambled.
2. Transfer eggs to the plate containing shrimps and then wipe clean the pan.
3. Return pan over high heat, add remaining oil, and when very hot, add green onions and cook for 15 seconds.

Adult + *Kid*:

1. Add cooked rice, stir until combined, and then cook for 2 minutes until hot; do not mix.
2. Then stir the rice, drizzle with soy sauce, add carrots and peas, eggs and shrimps, drizzle with sesame oil, and then toss until it is well mixed.
3. Cook the rice for 3 minutes until hot, then divide evenly among four plates and then serve.

Nutritional Information per Serving: Calories: *237.6 Cal;* Total Fat: *5.8 g;* Saturated Fat: *1.2 g;* Cholesterol: *168 mg;* Carbohydrates: *35.8 g;* Fiber: *1.3 g;* Sugar: *0.4 g;* Protein: *17.6 g;*

Meatloaf

Prep & cook time: 1 hour 10 minutes

Yield: 1 meatloaf

Ingredients:

- 1 pound ground beef
- ¼ cup breadcrumbs
- 1 pound ground pork
- 1 egg, at room temperature
- ¼ cup grated parmesan cheese

- 1/3 cup ketchup

Extra Ingredients:

- 1 ½ teaspoon salt
- 1 teaspoon ground black pepper

Directions:

Adult:

1. Switch on the oven, then set it to 375 degrees F and let it preheat.

Adult + *Kid*:

1. Take a large bowl, place all the Ingredients in it, and then stir until well mixed.

Adult:

1. Take a 9-by-13 inch baking pan, line it with a parchment sheet, and then grease it with oil.

Kid:

1. Spoon the meat mixture into the pan, press it and spread evenly, and spread some more ketchup on top.

Adult:

1. Place the baking pan containing meatloaf on the lower rack of the heated oven and then bake for 1 hour until cooked until thoroughly cooked.
2. When done, use the parchment sheet to take out the meatloaf, let it rest for 15 minutes, and then cut it into eight slices.
3. Serve straight away.

Nutritional Information per Serving: *Calories:* 331 Cal; *Total Fat:* 18 g; *Saturated Fat:* 6.4 g; *Cholesterol:* 123 mg; *Carbohydrates:* 14 g; *Fiber:* 1.2 g; *Sugar:* 6.1 g; *Protein:* 27 g;

Sloppy Joes

Prep & cook time: 40 minutes

Yield: 4 sloppy joes

Ingredients:

- 1 pound ground beef
- ½ of a medium zucchini
- 2 stalks of celery
- ½ of a medium green bell pepper
- 1/3 cup barbecue sauce
- 10 ounces tomato soup
- 4 whole-wheat burger buns

Extra Ingredients:

- 1 teaspoon salt
- ½ teaspoon ground black pepper
- 1 teaspoon paprika
- 1 tablespoon olive oil

Directions:

Adult:

1. Place zucchini in a food processor, add celery and bell pepper, and then puree for 30 seconds or more until smooth.
2. Take a large skillet pan, place it over medium-high heat, add oil, and let it heat for 2 minutes.

Adult + *Kid*:

1. Add blended vegetable mixture into the pan, stir until just mixed, and then cook for 3 to 5 minutes until most of the cooking liquid has evaporated.

2. Add beef into the pan, break it with the spoon, stir until well mixed with the vegetables and then stir in salt, black pepper, and paprika.

3. Cook the beef for 8 minutes until thoroughly cooked, add tomato soup and BBQ sauce, and then stir until combined.

4. Cook the mixture for 10 minutes until thickened, then remove the pan from heat and let the mixture stand for 1 minute.

5. Cut the bun in half lengthwise, ladle one-fourth of the meat sauce in it, and then serve.

Nutritional Information per Serving: Calories: *317 Cal*; Total Fat: *13.5 g*; Saturated Fat: *4.9 g*; Cholesterol: *63.5 mg*; Carbohydrates: *24 g*; Fiber: *1.5 g*; Sugar: *3.5 g*; Protein: *23.2 g*;

Honey-roasted carrots with rosemary

Prep & cook: 45 minutes

Serves: 4

Ingredients

- 2 tablespoons butter
- 2 tablespoons honey
- Flake salt, such as Maldon
- 2 to 3 bunches small carrots, scrubbed and greens trimmed, halved lengthwise if thick
- 2 fresh rosemary sprigs, quills stripped from stems and coarsely chopped
- Freshly ground black pepper

Directions

1. Preheat the oven to 425°F.

2. *Prepare the glaze.* In a small saucepan over medium heat, melt the butter. Add the honey, and whisk to dissolve. Season with a pinch of salt, and set aside.

3. Toss the Ingredients together. On a baking sheet, drizzle the honey mixture over the carrots, toss to coat, and scatter the chopped rosemary on top. Season with salt and pepper.

4. *Roast the carrots.* Bake for 30 to 35 minutes, or until the carrots are tender and caramelized in spots, rearranging them for even browning halfway through.

5. Serve. Transfer to a serving platter or plates and eat warm.

Summery corn and watermelon salad

Prep: 15 minutes

Serves: 4

Ingredients

- 5 fresh basil leaves
- ½ small watermelon, seeded, rind
- removed, cut into 1-inch cubes
- 2 ears fresh sweet corn, cooked and cut off the cob
- teaspoon ground sumac
- ¼ teaspoon ground cayenne
- Zest of ½ lemon
- Flake salt, such as Maldon

Directions

1. *Assemble the salad.* Transfer the cubed watermelon and any accumulated juices to a serving platter. Add the corn cut off the cobs (it is okay if there are rows of corn left intact; that is part of the fun). Sprinkle the sumac and cayenne over the mixture, followed by the lemon zest.

2. *Cut the basil into a chiffonade.* Do this immediately before serving the salad, as the edges of the basil will darken from being cut (known as oxidation). Stack the basil leaves on top of each other, and roll into a tight bundle. Slice your knife across the roll, creating very thin strips (called chiffonade). Fluff the chiffonade to separate the strips, and scatter onto the salad.

3. *Serve.* Season with salt, and serve immediately.

Balsamic-glazed carrots

Prep: 15 minutes

Serves: 4

Ingredients

- Kosher salt
- bunch multicolored carrots
- tablespoons extra-virgin olive oil
- Freshly ground black pepper
- tablespoon balsamic vinegar
- ½ cup chicken stock
- tablespoon unsalted butter

Directions

1. *Preparing the Ingredients.* Bring a medium pot of salted water to a boil. Prepare a bowl of ice water. Peel the carrots and trim and discard the tops. Add the carrots to the pot and cook until nearly tender, 2 minutes. Transfer to the bowl of ice water and let cool.

2. Drain the carrots and pat dry with a clean kitchen towel. In a large pan, heat the olive oil over medium heat. Add the carrots and season them with salt and pepper. Add the vinegar, shaking the pan to turn the carrots, and coat with the vinegar.

3. Add the stock and butter and cook until the liquid reduces to a glaze and the carrots are tender 5 to 7 minutes. Serve hot.

Panzanella salad

Prep: 25 minutes

Serves: 4

Ingredients

- loaf crusty bread, torn into bite-size
- chunks and left to dry out on a baking
- sheet for 1 to 2 days
- tablespoons olive oil, plus extra for
- soaking, drizzling, and frying
- Flake salt, such as Maldon
- Freshly ground black pepper
- 5 large heirloom tomatoes, cut into
- wedges

- 1½ cups Sun Gold tomatoes halved
- cups fresh basil leaves, rinsed and patted dry
- chives, finely chopped
- 2 teaspoons red wine vinegar

Directions

1. Preheat the oven to 425°F.
2. *Toast the bread.* Arrange the bread on a baking sheet, and drizzle with olive oil, and season with salt and pepper. Toast the bread in the oven until golden and crisp on the edges, turning once halfway through as needed, about 8 minutes total.
3. *Assemble the salad.* Arrange the tomatoes on a serving platter, alternating shapes, and colors. Add the basil, and nestle the crispy bread into the mixture, then scatter the chives all around.
4. *Make the dressing.* In a small bowl, whisk the olive oil and red wine vinegar to combine.
5. *Serve.* Drizzle the dressing over the salad, saving some for at the table, season with salt and pepper, and dig in.

Roasted baby fennel gratin

Prep: 40 minutes

Serves: 4

Ingredients

- 2 cups heavy cream
- cup fennel fronds
- tablespoon fennel seeds, toasted
- Kosher salt and freshly ground black pepper
- cup chopped baby fennel
- ½ cup grated Gruyère cheese
- ½ cup bread crumbs
  - teaspoon fennel pollen
- ¼ pound French ham, very thinly sliced

Directions

1. Preparing the Ingredients
2. Preheat the oven to 375°F.
3. In a small saucepan, combine the cream, fennel fronds, and fennel seeds and bring to a simmer over medium-high heat. Remove the pan from the heat, cover, and let steep for 20 minutes. Strain through a fine-mesh sieve, discard the solids, and season with salt and pepper.
4. Bake Arrange the chopped fennel in four small gratin dishes. Divide the infused cream among the dishes. Bake until the fennel is soft and about half the cream has been absorbed, 15 to 20 minutes.
5. In a small bowl, combine the Gruyère, bread crumbs, and fennel pollen. Sprinkle the bread crumb mixture over the fennel gratin and bake until the bread crumbs are golden, 10 minutes. Remove from the oven and scatter the ham over the tops. Let cool slightly and serve.

Kale chips

Prep: 30 minutes

Serves: 8

Ingredients

- 2 bunches kale, washed and dried
- 2 teaspoons olive oil, plus more if needed
- ½ teaspoon sea salt, plus more to taste
- ¼ teaspoon garlic powder (optional)
- ¼ cup grated Parmesan cheese (optional)

Directions

1. *Preheat the oven, and chop the vegetables.* Preheat the oven to 375°F. With a cutting board and a kid-safe knife, cut out the center stems of the kale. Roughly chop the kale leaves.

2. *Season the chips.* In a large bowl, combine the kale, olive oil, salt, and garlic (if using). Using a wooden spoon, mix until the kale is completely coated with the other Ingredients.

3. *Bake the chips.* Spread the kale on a baking sheet. The kale does not need to be in a single layer, since it will shrink as it cooks. Bake for 15 to 20 minutes, turning once or twice while cooking until the leaves are crisp on the edges and slightly browned. Cool, add Parmesan cheese (if using), toss, and serve.

Minty avocado-melon mix

Prep: 25 minutes

Serves: 4

Ingredients

- ⅓ cup plus 1 tablespoon olive oil, divided
- 2 limes, one juiced and one cut into wedges for serving
- ¼ cup chopped fresh mint
- Sea salt
- Freshly ground black pepper
- (8-ounce) block Haloumi cheese, sliced into ¼-inch slices
- Cantaloupe halved and seeded
- Avocados halved and pitted

Directions

1. Make the dressing. In a small bowl, stir together ⅓ cup of olive oil with the juice of 1 lime, mint, and salt and pepper to taste. Set aside.

2. Fry the cheese. In a small cast-iron skillet over medium-high heat, heat the remaining 1 tablespoon of olive oil. Add the cheese slices, and lower the heat to medium. Moisture from the cheese can cause the oil to spatter, so be careful as you lay them in. Sear the cheese for a few minutes—you should hear them sizzle. Flip to the second side when the first is caramelized and browned. The second side takes only a couple of minutes. Transfer to a serving platter.

3. Prepare the melon. Use a melon baller to make spheres from the cantaloupe's flesh, and then arrange them on the platter beside the Haloumi.

4. Prepare the avocado. Repeat the process with the avocados. Do this just before serving time so that the avocado doesn't oxidize, and squeeze a wedge or two of fresh lime juice over the avocado spheres, tossing to coat.

5. Serve. Layer the mixture of avocado and melon balls next to the Haloumi, and spoon the chopped mint dressing overall. Serve with the remaining lime wedges, and eat immediately.

Shaved fennel salad

Prep: 10 minutes

Serves: 4

Ingredients

- 3 tablespoons olive oil
- tablespoon champagne vinegar
- fennel bulb, very thinly sliced
- tablespoons chopped fennel fronds
- ½ grapefruit, segmented and chopped
- Kosher salt and freshly ground black pepper

Directions

1. Preparing the Ingredients
2. In a large bowl, whisk together the olive oil and vinegar.
3. Add the sliced fennel, fennel fronds, and grapefruit and toss to coat. Season with salt and pepper and serve.

Grainy mustard-potato salad

Prep: 20 minutes

Serves: 4

Ingredients

- 6 medium Yukon gold potatoes, scrubbed and cut into chunky wedges
- 3 medium Red Bliss potatoes, scrubbed and cut into chunky wedges
- 4 to 5 tablespoons olive oil
- 2 tablespoons whole-grain mustard
- tablespoon capers, well-rinsed and
- chopped
- shallot, sliced thin
- tablespoons dill, torn into small sprigs
- Sea salt
- Freshly ground black pepper

Directions

1. *Boil the potatoes.* In a large saucepan, cover the potatoes with water and gently boil them for 8 to 10 minutes, until fork-tender. Drain the potatoes in a colander, and transfer to a large bowl.
2. *Dress the potatoes.* In a large bowl, toss the olive oil, mustard, capers, and shallot to combine with the potatoes.
3. *Serve.* Once the potato mixture has cooled to room temperature, add the dill sprigs, and toss again. Season to taste with salt and pepper. Enjoy warm, at room temperature, or chilled.

Broccoli rabe puree

Prep: 15 minutes

Serves: 4

Ingredients

- Kosher salt

- bunch broccoli rabe
- tablespoons extra-virgin olive oil
- Freshly ground black pepper

Directions

1. Preparing the Ingredients
2. Bring a large pot of salted water to a boil. Add the broccoli rabe and cook until just tender, 3 to 4 minutes.
3. Transfer the broccoli rabe to a blender, reserving the cooking liquid. Add the olive oil and blend on high until completely smooth. If the purée is too thick, add some cooking liquid, 1 tablespoon at a time, until the purée is your desired texture. Season with salt and pepper. Serve.

Turkey & Cucumber Salad Wraps

Prep: 30 minutes

Serves: 4

Ingredients

- ¼ cup mayonnaise
- ¼ cup mango chutney
- ground black pepper
- 2 cups chopped cantaloupe (about ½ medium cantaloupe)
- ½ small English (seedless) cucumber, chopped
- ½ cup packed fresh cilantro leaves
- 4 burrito size flour tortillas
- 2 cups mixed greens
- pound thinly sliced reduced-sodium deli-smoked turkey

Directions

1. *Preparing the Ingredients.* In a large bowl, combine mayonnaise, chutney, and pepper. Add cantaloupe, cucumber, and cilantro, tossing to combine.
2. Working with 1 tortilla at a time, place about ¾ cup cantaloupe mixture, ½ cup greens, and ¼ pound turkey in the center of the tortilla. Fold in sides and roll tightly around the filling. Serve.

Nutty parmesan-kale salad

Prep: 25 minutes

Serves: 4

Ingredients

- A bunch lacinato kale, also known as
- 1 Tuscan or dinosaur kale, rinsed, ends trimmed
- Zest and juice of 1 lemon
- 2 tablespoons olive oil
- Flake salt, such as Maldon
- 1 Freshly ground black pepper
- 2 cup hazelnuts
- ½ cup shaved Parmigiano-Reggiano

Directions

1. *Chop the kale.* Gather the kale into a tight bunch or stack the leaves on top of each

other, and slice into very thin strips, about ⅛ inch wide. Transfer to a large bowl.

2. *Dress the salad.* Add the lemon zest and juice and the olive oil to the bowl, season with salt and pepper, and toss to combine. Taste and adjust seasoning, and set aside.

3. *Prepare the nuts.* Toast the hazelnuts for 5 minutes or until fragrant. When cool enough to handle, gently rub off their skins. Arrange the nuts on a cutting board. Coarsely crush them by leaning your weight onto the side of a chef's knife placed on them. Transfer nuts to the toaster oven tray and toast again until golden, about 3 minutes more. Empty the nuts into a small serving bowl. At the table, scatter the hazelnuts and shaved Parm over the salad, and serve immediately.

Brussels sprout stir-fry

Prep: 15 minutes

Serves: 4

Ingredients

- 1 tablespoon grapeseed oil
- 2 cups Brussels sprouts, trimmed and halved, or quartered, if large
- Kosher salt and freshly ground black pepper
- ½ onion, thinly sliced
- ½ cup kalamata olives, pitted and chopped
- ¼ teaspoon crushed red pepper flakes
- ¼ teaspoon cayenne
- ½ cup very thinly sliced fennel
- tablespoons fresh lemon juice

Directions

1. *Preparing the Ingredients.* In a large pan, heat the grapeseed oil over medium-high heat. Add the Brussels sprouts and season lightly with salt and black pepper. Cook, stirring occasionally, until caramelized and tender, about 4 minutes. Add the onion, olives, red pepper flakes, and cayenne and cook until the onion softens, 1 to 2 minutes. Stir in the fennel and cook just until warmed through.

2. Remove the pan from the heat, add the lemon juice, and season with more salt and black pepper. Serve hot.

Sauteed broccolini

Prep: 15 minutes

Serves: 4

Ingredients

- 1 pound Broccolini, tough bottoms trimmed
- 2 tablespoons extra-virgin olive oil
- 1 shallot, minced
- 1 garlic cloves, minced
- ½ teaspoons crushed red pepper flakes
- A pinch of Kosher salt
- 2 tablespoons unsalted butter

Directions

1. Preparing the Ingredients
2. In a large bowl, combine the Broccolini, olive oil, shallot, garlic, and red pepper flakes. Season with salt and toss to coat evenly.

3. In a large sauté pan, melt the butter over medium-high heat. Add the Broccolini and cook, flipping once or twice, until tender, 4 to 6 minutes. Serve.

Egg salad and toast points

Prep: 25 minutes

Serves: 4

Ingredients

- 8 eggs
- Ice water
- 4 slices crusty bread, such as sourdough or seeded wheat, crusts removed, and cut diagonally in half, into triangles
- 2 tablespoons mayonnaise
- 2 teaspoons Dijon mustard
- teaspoon freshly squeezed lemon juice
- celery stalk, finely chopped
- tablespoon finely chopped cornichons
- tablespoon finely chopped parsley
- Sea salt
- Freshly ground black pepper

Directions

1. Cook the eggs. In a saucepan large enough for the eggs to sit in a single layer, bring to a boil enough water to submerge the eggs by at least 1 inch. Carefully lower the eggs into the water, return to a boil, and simmer for 10 minutes. Have a large bowl filled with ice water nearby.

2. Transfer and peel the eggs. Use a slotted spoon to transfer the eggs to the water to chill them for peeling. Let the eggs sit in the ice bath until cool to the touch. Tap the eggshell on your work surface, turning it and cracking it throughout. Peel the shells and discard.

3. Toast the bread. Toast the bread pieces in the toaster oven until golden and crisp. Transfer to individual plates or a serving dish.

4. Assemble the salad. In a medium bowl, use a fork or potato masher to mash the hard-cooked eggs, combining them with the mayonnaise, mustard, and lemon juice. You may opt to keep the consistency chunky, or for a creamier consistency, mash until well combined.

5. Finish assembling. Add the celery, cornichons, and parsley, and season with salt and pepper. Stir gently to combine.

6. Serve with the toast points chilled or at room temperature. Any leftovers will keep, sealed in the refrigerator, for up to 4 days.

Cucumber and tomato salad

Prep: 5 minutes

Serves: 4

Ingredients

- ⅔ cup of rice vinegar
- ¼ cup of sugar
- 2 teaspoons kosher salt
- 2 English cucumbers
- 2 cups cherry tomatoes, halved

Directions

1. Preparing the Ingredients
2. In a medium bowl, whisk together the vinegar, sugar, and salt. Whisk until the sugar and salt have dissolved.
3. Slice the cucumbers lengthwise as thinly as possible, and then cut each slice lengthwise again to create very thin strips. Place the cucumber strips in a large bowl. Add the cherry tomatoes and the dressing. Toss gently to evenly coat and serve.

Roasted cauliflower with dipping sauce

Prep: 1 hour 5 minutes

Serves: 4

Ingredients

FOR THE CAULIFLOWER

- 1½ cups dry white wine or white wine vinegar
- 6 cups of water
- ⅓ cup olive oil, plus more for serving
- 3 tablespoons kosher salt
- 3 tablespoons freshly squeezed lemon juice
- 2 tablespoons orange juice
- 2 tablespoons butter
- tablespoon crushed red pepper flakes
- Pinch black peppercorns
- bay leaf
- head cauliflower, stem trimmed
- Flake salt, such as Maldon, for serving

FOR THE SAUCE

- ½ cup crème fraîche
- 3 tablespoons nonfat Greek yogurt
- ¼ cup finely shredded Parmigiano-Reggiano
- 3 teaspoons capers, rinsed and chopped
- Freshly ground black pepper

Directions

1. *Poach the cauliflower.* In a Dutch oven or other heavy-bottomed pot over high heat, bring the wine, water, olive oil, kosher salt, lemon juice, orange juice, butter, red pepper flakes, peppercorns, and bay leaf to a boil. Add the cauliflower, then reduce the heat to simmer. Turn occasionally, using a pair of serving spoons to submerge each side in the poaching liquid, until a knife easily inserts into the center, 15 to 20 minutes.
2. Preheat the oven to 475°F.
3. Make the dipping sauce. In a small bowl, mix the crème fraîche, Greek yogurt, cheese, and capers, and season with pepper. Set aside.
4. Roast the cauliflower. Using tongs or the serving spoons, transfer cauliflower to a roasting pan. Roast, rotating the sheet if browning unevenly, until deep golden and crispy in parts, about 35 minutes.
5. Serve. Bring the roasted cauliflower to the table, set on a trivet, and serve directly from the roasting pan with the dipping sauce—and a spoon to dispense it—alongside.

Green papaya and bell pepper salad

Prep: 10 minutes

Serves: 4-6

Ingredients

- Zest of 2 key limes
- cup fresh key lime juice
- teaspoons minced garlic
- tablespoon molasses
- tablespoon finely grated fresh ginger
- teaspoons kosher salt
- teaspoon freshly ground black pepper
- cups extra-virgin olive oil
- green (unripe) papaya
- yellow or red bell pepper, cut into very thin strips

Directions

1. *Preparing the Ingredients.* In a medium bowl, whisk together the lime zest, lime juice, garlic, molasses, ginger, salt, and black pepper. While whisking, gradually add the olive oil in a thin, steady stream.

2. Peel and thinly slice the papaya, discarding the seeds and inner membrane, and place in a large serving bowl. Add the bell pepper. Pour in about half the dressing, toss gently, and then add more dressing if needed to coat the papaya and bell pepper. Serve.

Roasted brussels sprouts and shallots

Prep: 40 minutes

Serves: 4

Ingredients

- 1½ pounds Brussels sprouts, trimmed and halved
- 6 shallots, quartered
- 3 tablespoons olive oil
- Sea salt
- Freshly ground black pepper
- lemon, cut into wedges, for serving

Directions

1. Arrange oven racks and preheat oven

2. Place one oven rack in the top third of the oven and another in the bottom third, then preheat the oven to 450°F.

3. Prep the veggie mixture. On two baking sheets, toss the Brussels sprouts and shallots with the olive oil, placing most of the Brussels halves cut-side down. Season with salt and pepper.

4. Roast the vegetables. Swap the pans halfway through, and use tongs to turn the veggies over for even roasting. Cook until caramelized and tender, 25 to 30 minutes.

5. Serve. Transfer the Brussels sprouts and shallots to a serving dish, with lemon wedges to squeeze at the table.

Summer strawberry salad

Prep: 10 minutes

Serves: 4

Ingredients

- 2 heads red-leaf lettuce

- ½ cup plus 2 tablespoons olive oil
- Kosher salt and freshly ground black pepper
- cup strawberries, sliced
- cup peeled orange segments
- ¼ cup chopped fresh flat-leaf parsley
- tablespoons balsamic vinegar
- tablespoon cola

Directions

1. Preparing the Ingredients
2. Heat a grill to high or a grill pan over high heat.
3. Remove the large outer leaves from the red-leaf lettuce and cut each head in half lengthwise through the bottom stem. Brush the lettuce halves with 2 tablespoons of the olive oil. Grill until lightly charred, flipping once, about 2 minutes per side. Transfer to a plate, season with salt and pepper, and let cool. Cut or tear the lettuce leaves into bite-size pieces and place them in a large bowl. Add the strawberries, orange segments, and parsley.
4. In a small bowl, whisk together the vinegar, cola, and the remaining ½ cup olive oil. Season with salt and pepper. Pour the dressing over the salad and toss gently to coat. Serve immediately.

Chapter 4:

Cookies Recipes

Honey Cookies

Prep & cook Time: *50 minutes*

Servings: 10

Ingredients:

- 1 ½ cups of shortening
- 2 cups of light brown sugar
- 2 eggs
- ½ cup of honey
- 1 teaspoon lemon extract
- 4 ½ cups flour
- 2 teaspoon. baker's style baking soda
- 2 teaspoon baker's style baking powder
- 1 teaspoon salt
- 1 teaspoon powdered cinnamon

Directions:

1. In a bowl, add in the shortening and light brown sugar. Beat with an electric mixer until fluffy inconsistency. Add in the eggs, honey, and lemon extract.
2. Continue to beat until creamy inconsistency. Add in the flour, salt, powdered cinnamon, baking powder, and soda. Continue to mix until just mixed.
3. Shape into 12 rolls and slice into ¼ inch thick slices. Place onto baking sheets.
4. In the oven, bake for 10 to 15 minutes or until golden.

NUTRITION: Calories: 230 Fat: 10g Protein: 9g Carbs: 24g

Spiced Oatmeal Cookies

Prep & cook Time: 40 minutes

Servings: 24

Ingredients:

- 1 cup of shortening
- 2 cups of light brown sugar
- 2 eggs
- 2 Tablespoon of whole milk
- 2 1/2 cups of flour
- 2 cups of old fashioned oats
- 1 teaspoon of baker's style baking soda
- 1 teaspoon of salt
- 1 teaspoon of powdered cinnamon

Directions:

1. Add in the shortening and light brown sugar in a bowl. Beat with an electric mixer until creamy inconsistency.
2. Add in the eggs and whole milk. Beat again to incorporate.
3. In a separate bowl, add in the flour, baking soda, salt, and powdered cinnamon.
4. Pour into the shortening mix. Stir again until just mixed.
5. Drop by the tablespoon onto baking sheets.
6. Bake in the oven for 10 to 15 minutes at 350 degrees or until baked through.
7. Remove and cool completely before serving.

NUTRITION: Calories: 230 Fat: 12g Protein: 9g Carbs: 24g

Double Butterscotch Cookies

Prep & cook Time: 4 hours 50 minutes

Servings: 42

Ingredients:

- 1/2 cup of butter, soft
- 1/2 cup of shortening
- 4 cups of light brown sugar
- 4 eggs
- 1 Tablespoon. of pure vanilla
- 6 cups of flour
- 3 teaspoon of baker's style baking soda
- 3 teaspoon of cream of tartar
- 1 teaspoon of salt
- 10-ounce pack of English toffee bits
- 1 cup of pecans, chopped

Directions:

1. Add in the soft butter, shortening, and light brown sugar in a bowl. Beat with an electric mixer until sand-like inconsistency.
2. Add in the eggs and pure vanilla.
3. Continue to mix until evenly incorporated.
4. In a bowl, add in the flour, baker's style baking soda, cream of tartar and, dash of salt. Stir well to mix.
5. Add into the brown sugar mix. Stir well to mix.
6. Add in the English toffee bits and chopped pecans. Stir well to mix.
7. Shape into rolls. Slice the rolls in half and place onto a baking sheet.
8. Cover and place into the fridge to chill for 4 hours or until firm.
9. In the oven, bake for 10 to 12 minutes at 375 degrees or until light brown.

NUTRITION: Calories: 235 Fat: 12g Protein: 10g Carbs: 22g

Jelly Bean Cookies

Prep & cook Time: 35 minutes

Servings: 32

Ingredients:

- 1/2 cup of shortening

- 3/4 cup of white sugar
- 1 egg
- 2 Tablespoon of 2 percent milk
- 1 teaspoon of pure vanilla
- 1 1/2 cups of flour
- 1 1/4 teaspoon of baker's style baking powder
- 1/2 teaspoon of salt
- 3/4 cup of jelly beans

Directions:

1. Heat the oven to 30 degrees. Add in the shortening and white sugar in a bowl. Beat well until evenly mixed.
2. Add in the egg, 2 percent milk, and pure vanilla. Continue to beat until creamy inconsistency.
3. In a separate bowl, add in the flour, baking powder and salt. Stir to mix and pour into the sugar mix. Stir well until just mixed.
4. Drop the dough by the tablespoon onto baking sheets lined with sheets of parchment paper. Press the jelly beans into the dough.
5. Place into the oven to bake for 8 to 10 minutes or until the edges begin to turn light brown.
6. Remove and set onto a wire rack to cool completely before serving.

NUTRITION: Calories: 232 Fat: 10g Protein: 8g Carbs: 20g

Classic Peanut Butter Cookies

Prep & cook Time: 40 minutes

Servings: 36

Ingredients:

- 1 cup of shortening
- 1 cup of smooth peanut butter
- 1 cup of white sugar
- 1 cup of light brown sugar
- 3 eggs
- 3 cups of flour
- 2 teaspoon of baker's style baking soda
- 1/4 teaspoon of salt

Directions:

1. Preheat the oven to 375 degrees.
2. In a bowl, add in the shortening, smooth peanut butter, white sugar, and light brown sugar.
3. Beat with an electric mixer until smooth inconsistency. Add in the eggs and continue to beat until evenly mixed.
4. In a separate bowl, add in the flour, salt, and baking soda. Stir well to mix.
5. Add into the shortening mixture and stir well until just mixed.
6. Divide the dough into 1 ½ inch balls. Place onto a baking sheet. Flatten slightly.
7. In the oven, bake for 10 to 15 minutes.
8. Remove and transfer onto a wire rack to cool before serving.

NUTRITION: Calories: 222 Fat: 10g Protein: 9g Carbs: 24g

Blueberry Bars

Prep & cook Time: 55 minutes

Servings: 4

Ingredients:

- 3 cups of blueberries, fresh or frozen
- ½ cup of White Sugar
- 3 tablespoon Lemon Juice
- 3 tablespoon Water
- 4 teaspoon Cornstarch
- 2 cups of Rolled Oats
- 1 teaspoon Cinnamon
- 1 cup of Light Brown Sugar
- ½ teaspoon Baking Soda
- ¾ cup of Butter softened.

Directions:

1. Gas Mark 5 and line a 9" square baking tin. Heat the blueberries, lemon juice, water, and sugar in a saucepan.
2. Heat until it reaches a boil and cook for 10 minutes until the blueberries are syrupy and broken down a little. Stir in the cornstarch and cook for a further few minutes to thicken. Allow to cooling completely.
3. In a bowl mix all the other Ingredients. Pat half of the mix into the bottom of the baking tin and press down firmly.
4. Pour the cooled blueberry mixture on top. Finish off by sprinkling over the remaining oat mix and press down a little.
5. Bake for 30-40 minutes until crisp and golden.

NUTRITION: Calories: 235 Fat: 15g Protein: 7g Carbs: 25g

Superseded Slice

Prep & cook Time: 35 minutes

Servings: 9

Ingredients:

- ¾ cup/6oz Butter
- ¼ cup of Honey
- 1/3 cup of Dark Brown Sugar
- ½ cup of Pumpkin Seeds
- ½ cup of Sunflower Seeds
- 4 tablespoon Sesame Seeds
- 1/2 cup of Rolled Oats
- 1 tablespoon Oat brown

Directions:

1. Preheat the oven to 375°F/190°C/Gas Mark 5 and line a 9" square baking tin.
2. Melt the butter, syrup, and sugar together.

3. Mix in all the Ingredients well.
4. Press into the baking tray. For 20-25 minutes, bake until crunchy and golden on top.

NUTRITION: Calories: 240 Fat: 10g Protein: 8g Carbs: 20g

Garlic Dough Balls

Prep & cook Time: 20 minutes

Servings: 24

Ingredients:

- 3 cups of Strong Flour
- 1 tablespoon Dried Yeast
- 1 teaspoon Salt
- 2 Garlic Cloves, crushed
- 1 tablespoon Garlic Oil
- 1 teaspoon Sugar
- 300ml Warm Milk

Directions:

1. Add all of the Ingredients together and either knead using a bread hook on a processor or flour a surface and knead by hand.
2. After 8-10 minutes and when the dough is soft and elastic, leave in an oiled bowl, covered, and in a warm place, prove for 1 hour.
3. Give the dough a good knead to remove the air and then roll into approximately 24 balls.

4. In the oven, place on the baking tray and bake for 15-20 minutes until risen and cooked.

NUTRITION: Calories: 222 Fat: 10g Protein: 9g Carbs: 24g

Homemade Dry Pebble Cookies

Prep & cook Time: 40 minutes

Servings: 40

Ingredients:

- 100 g flour (top grade or half with whole grain)
- 30 g cornstarch
- 2 tablespoons vegetable oil (Odorless)
- 2 tablespoons sugar
- 1 tablespoon milk
- 1 egg
- 1 teaspoon vanilla sugar
- 1/2 teaspoon disintegrant
- 1 pinch salt

Directions:

1. Mix flour, starch, and disintegrant. Put all other components in the container - oil, sugar, vanilla sugar, milk, egg, and salt.
2. Beat slightly with a crown until you have a light, uniform foam.
3. Gradually pour in the dry mixture, first mixing with a spoon. Then use your hands to mix a little.

4. The dough will appear to be soft, flexible, and not sticky, but also not hard.

5. Then the dough needs to be finely rolled, which is quite difficult because it contains little fat. I roll directly on an inverted tray.

6. This is very appropriate because you don't need to carry the cookies anywhere, and it doesn't lose its shape. If desired, it is possible to roll out on the table and transfer cookies to the pan.

7. Rolling the dough very fine, about 2 mm is very important. This way, the cookies will turn out to be crispy (it should be taken into account that the cookies will still rise due to the disintegrate).

8. Cut cookies with molds or cut them into squares. Stab each with a fork.

9. Put in a pre-heated oven at 180 degrees C. Bake for about 10-15 minutes. As soon as the cookies are slightly stuck, they are ready!

NUTRITION: Calories: 222 Fat: 8g Protein: 7g Carbs: 18g

Mushroom Cookies

Prep & cook Time: 45 minutes

Servings: 8

Ingredients:

- 250-300 g butter
- 1 glass powdered sugar
- 2 eggs
- 2/3 tablespoon cocoa
- 4 glasses corn starch
- ½ glass flour
- 1 teaspoon baking soda

Directions:

1. Beat softened butter in a bowl with powdered sugar and then add eggs. Combine flour, starch, and soda in a bowl.

2. Gradually add to the oil-egg mixture, mixing to form a dough.

3. Separate the dough into walnut-size. Pour cocoa into a bowl. Take a clean, dry, empty bottle. Dip the neck bottle into the cocoa. Form a ball from the dough and slightly press into the neck of the bottle so that part of the dough is in the neck of the bottle.

4. Once taken out, a mushroom shape is formed.

5. Heat the oven to 180 degrees. Cover the pan with baking paper.

6. Place "mushrooms" on the pan, leaving space between them (in the process of baking, the volume will increase).

7. Bake for 20-25 minutes.

NUTRITION: Calories: 222 Fat: 8g Protein: 9g Carbs: 22g

Madeleine Cookies

Prep & cook Time: 40 minutes

Servings: 10

Ingredients:

- 2 eggs (large)
- 150g flour
- 100g sugar

- 120g butter

Directions:

1. Whisk the eggs with sugar into a light mixture. Pour in flour and mix gently.
2. Add the melted butter and mix again until a uniform mixture is obtained.
3. Roll out the dough into molds and bake for 10-12 minutes at 200 degrees C.
4. Different flavorings can be added to the dough.

NUTRITION: Calories: 230 Fat: 10g Protein: 8g Carbs: 25g

"Peach" Cookies

Prep & cook Time: 45 minutes

Servings: 12

Ingredients:

Dough:

- 60g butter or margarine
- 3 tablespoons Sour cream 15-20 percent
- 200g sugar
- 1 bag vanillin
- 2 eggs
- 1 bag or 1-1.5 teaspoons disintegrant
- 500g flour

Stuffing:

- 1 can cooked thickening
- 1/2 packs (100g) butter
- Crumbs (flesh cut from peach)
- Coating:
- Beetroots, carrot juice
- Sugar

Directions:

1. Dough: Whip eggs with sugar and added softened butter. Add sour cream and vanillin. Shake.
2. Mix flour with disintegrate, sift and add to the dough. Knead the dough, then let rest.
3. Roll into a sausage (not thin). Cut into uniform pieces and make balls from the dough.
4. Cut each ball in half and make halves for the peaches. Place ready-made halves on a pan covered with parchment paper.
5. Bake for 15 minutes at 180-200 degrees C. After the halves have cooled down a little bit, take a knife and cut out a bit of the middle from the flat side.
6. In the meantime, make the cream.

Stuffing: Whip soft butter with boiled, thickened crumbs (flesh cut from peach).

7. Take two halves, and starting with the middle, oil the edges to connect.
8. Put in the refrigerator to freeze the filling.
9. Decorate the cookies with beetroot juice or carrots, and sprinkle with sugar.

NUTRITION: Calories: 230 Fat: 10g Protein: 9g Carbs: 24g

Flour Cookies

Prep & cook Time: 35 minutes

Servings: 15

Ingredients:

- 250 g butter
- ½ glass powdered sugar
- 1/3 glass refined vegetable oil
- 4 tablespoons starch
- glasses flour
- 1 pack (10g) vanilla sugar

Directions:

1. Put butter (room temperature), powdered sugar, and vegetable oil in a bowl.
2. Beat well with a mixer. Add starch and mix with mixer.
3. Add a glass of flour and mix with a mixer. Add another glass of flour, this time mixing with a spoon.
4. Put 1 glass of flour on the table, and place dough on top. Mix the dough with your hands until it is uniform.
5. Add the last half of a glass of flour and continue mixing.
6. Divide the dough into 3 parts. Roll each part into a flask and cut it into pieces with a knife.
7. Place pieces of dough on a pan, covered with parchment.
8. Bake at 150°C for 30 to 60 minutes, depending on the oven.
9. Pour powdered sugar on top of slightly cooled cookies.

NUTRITION: Calories: 220 Fat: 10g Protein: 10g Carbs: 22g

Snowball Christmas Cookies

Prep & cook Time: 45 minutes

Servings: 10

Ingredients:

- 250 g Butter
- 130 g Powdered sugar
- 100 g Flour
- 250 g Starch
- 50 g Ground almonds
- 1 pack Vanilla sugar

Directions:

1. Beat softened butter, sift powdered sugar, and vanilla sugar. Sift the flour and starch, mix, and add to the butter with almonds.
2. Knead the sand dough. From the dough, roll and cut into circles.
3. First, give a little shape to each ball, and then press slightly with a fork to make a pattern.
4. Spread the cookies onto a pan covered with baking paper, leaving a distance between the cookies, as they will slightly increase.
5. Bake at 180°C and bake for 20 minutes; the cookies should not get dark.
6. Cool slightly and sprinkle with powdered sugar. Store in a closed container.
7. Cookies must be refrigerated for at least one day, and they will become even tastier.

NUTRITION: Calories: 230 Fat: 10g Protein: 8g Carbs: 20g

Coffee Gingersnap Cookies

Prep & cook Time: 1 hour 45 minutes

Servings: 6

Ingredients:

- 1/2 cup butter, softened
- 1/4 cup coconut oil
- 1 cup light brown sugar
- 1 egg
- 1 teaspoon vanilla extract
- 2 cups flour
- 1 teaspoon baking soda
- 1/4 teaspoon salt
- 1 teaspoon cinnamon powder
- 1 teaspoon ground ginger
- 1/2 teaspoon ground cardamom
- 2 teaspoons instant coffee

Directions:

1. In a bowl, mix the butter, coconut oil, and brown sugar until fluffy and creamy.
2. Add vanilla and egg then mix well.
3. Fold in the rest of the Ingredients then drop a spoonful of batter on a baking sheet lined with baking paper.
4. Bake for 15 minutes or until fragrant and crisp.
5. Serve the cookies chilled.

NUTRITION: Calories: 142 Fat: 7.7g Protein: 1.7g Carbohydrates: 16.8g

Peanut Butter Nutella Cookies

Prep & cook Time: 1 hour 45minutes

Servings: 20

Ingredients:

- ½ cup peanut butter, softened
- 1 ½ cups flour
- ¼ cup butter, softened
- ½ teaspoon baking soda
- ½ cup dark brown sugar
- 1 egg
- 1 teaspoon vanilla extract
- ½ teaspoon baking powder
- ½ cup Nutella
- ¼ teaspoon salt

Directions:

1. Mix the butter, peanut butter, and sugar in a bowl until creamy and fluffy.
2. Add the egg and vanilla and give it a good mix.
3. Fold in the flour, baking soda, baking powder, and salt.
4. Add the Nutella and swirl it into the batter.
5. Drop spoonful's of batter on a baking sheet lined with baking paper.

6. In the preheated oven, bake the cookies at 350F for 15 minutes or until golden brown on the edges.

7. Serve the cookies chilled.

NUTRITION: Calories: 120 Fat: 6.5g Protein: 3.0g Carbohydrates: 13.2g

Honey Lemon Cookies

Prep & cook Time: 1 hour 45 minutes

Servings: 40

Ingredients:

- 3 cups flour
- 1 teaspoon baking soda
- ½ teaspoon salt
- 1 cup butter, softened
- ¾ cup white sugar
- ¼ cup honey
- 1 lemon, zested and juiced
- 1 egg

Directions:

1. In a bowl, sieve the baking soda, flour, salt.
2. In a different bowl, mix the butter, sugar, and honey and mix well.
3. Mix in the lemon zest and juice, and the egg.
4. Fold in the flour mixture then roll the dough into a thin sheet over a floured working surface.
5. Cut the cookies with a cutter.

6. Place the cookies in the preheated oven at 350F for 10-15 minutes or until golden brown on the edges.

7. Serve the cookies chilled.

NUTRITION: Calories: 97 Fat: 4.8g Protein: 1.2g Carbohydrates: 12.8g

Butter Vanilla Cookies

Prep & cook Time: 1 hour 15 minutes

Servings: 30

Ingredients:

- 2 cups flour
- ¼ cup cornstarch
- ¼ teaspoon salt
- ½ cup powdered sugar
- 1 cup butter, softened
- 1 egg
- 1 tablespoon vanilla extract

Directions:

1. Mix in the sugar and butter until fluffy and creamy.
2. Add the vanilla and egg and mix well.
3. Fold in the flour, cornstarch, and salt and mix well.
4. Drop spoonsful of batter on a baking sheet lined with baking paper.
5. Bake in the preheated oven at 350F for 10-15 minutes or until golden brown on the edges.
6. Serve the cookies chilled.

NUTRITION: Calories: 100 Fat: 6.4g Protein: 1.1g Carbohydrates: 9.4g

Fudgy Chocolate Cookies

Prep & cook Time: 1 hour 45 minutes

Servings: 10

Ingredients:

- 1 ½ cups dark chocolate chips
- ½ cup butter
- 2 eggs
- ½ cup light brown sugar
- 2 tablespoons white sugar
- 1 teaspoon vanilla extract
- 2/3 cup flour
- 1 teaspoon baking powder
- ¼ teaspoon salt

Directions:

1. Melt the butter and chocolate in a heat-resistant bowl over a hot water bath.
2. Mix the eggs and sugars in a bowl until fluffy and pale.
3. Stir in the chocolate and mix with a spatula.
4. Fold in the baking powder, flour, and salt then drop a spoonful of batter in a baking sheet lined with baking paper.
5. In the preheated oven, bake the cookies at 350F for 12-14 minutes.
6. Serve the cookies chilled.

NUTRITION: Calories: 82 Fat: 5.0g Protein: 1.1g Carbohydrates: 9.4g

CHAPTER 5:

Cakes Recipes

Carrot cakes with Orange and Honey Syrup

Prep & cook time: 35 minutes

Serves: 12

Ingredients

- 175g light muscovado sugar
- 200g self-rising flour
- 1 tbsp bicarbonate of soda
- 2 tbsp mixed spice
- 1 orange, zested and juiced
- 2 eggs
- 150ml sunflower oil
- 50g natural yogurt
- 200g carrots, peeled and grated

For the syrup and icing

- 50 ml runny honey
- 150g mascarpone
- 100g thick natural yogurt
- 75g icing sugar sieved
- Edible flowers or orange zest for garnish

Directions

1. Preheat the oven to 350°F. Grease muffin tins with oil then set aside.
2. Mix sugar, flour bicarbonate, spice mix, and orange zest in a mixing bowl.
3. In a separate bowl, whisk together eggs, sunflower oil, and yogurt until well combined.
4. Stir in the wet Ingredients into the dry Ingredients along with the carrots.
5. Divide the mixture among the tins then bakes for 22 minutes. Turn the cake out on a cooling rack and leave them to cool.
6. Meanwhile, heat honey and orange juice in a saucepan. Let it boil then simmer until it turns syrupy. Spoon the syrup on each cake and let it cool.
7. Make the icing by mixing mascarpone, natural yogurt, and icing sugar until well mixed. Swirl the icing on the cakes then garnish with flowers.
8. Serve and enjoy.

Nutritional Information: Calories 356, Total Fat 20g, Saturated Fat 6g, Total Carbs 39g, Net Carbs 37g, Protein 4g, Sugar 27g, Fiber 1g, salt 0.5g

Little pistachio cakes

Prep & cook time: 40 minutes

Serves: 12

Ingredients

- 175g butter, lightly salted
- 75g plain flour
- 140g pistachios plus a few for garnish
- 1 tbsp baking powder
- 175g golden caster sugar
- 2 tbsp vanilla extract
- 2 tbsp milk

For the icing

- 290g tub cream cheese
- 50g butter, lightly salted
- 100g icing sugar

Directions

1. Preheat oven to 350°F. Grease muffin tins with oil then dust with flour and set aside.
2. Place the pistachios in a food processor and pulse until fine but not greasy.
3. Add the rest of the cake Ingredients and pulse until creamy.
4. Scoop the mixture into the muffin tins up to two-thirds full. Bake for 15 minutes or until firm. let cool on a cooling rack.
5. Meanwhile, make the icing. Add 3 tbsp of cream cheese and butter in a small bowl then use a hand mixer to blend until smooth.
6. Add the remaining cream cheese and icing sugar then continue blending until smooth. Transfer into a piping bag.
7. Pipe the icing on the cakes then sprinkle with chopped pistachios.
8. Serve and enjoy or preserve up to 3 days.

Nutritional Information: Calories 444, Total Fat 33g, Saturated Fat 18g, Total Carbs 30g, Net Carbs 29g, Protein 5g, Sugar 24g, Fiber 1g, salt 0.6g

Cauliflower cheesecake

Prep time: 35 minutes

Serves: 4

Ingredients

- Oil for greasing
- 1/2 head cauliflower, cut into florets
- 1 slice brown bread, rip into chunks
- 1 egg
- 50g cheddar, grated
- A few chives snipped

Directions

1. Preheat oven to 350°F. Line a baking tray with parchment paper or foil. Brush with oil.
2. Place the cauliflower in a steamer basket over boiling water and cook for 8 minutes or until tender.
3. Pulse the bread in a food processor then add the cooked cauliflower, bread, egg, cheese, chives, and black pepper. Continue to pulse until a chunky consistency is achieved.

4. Divide the mixture into 8 patties and arrange them on the baking tray. Bake for 20 minutes or until golden and starts to crisp.
5. Serve and enjoy.

Nutritional Information: Calories 103, Total Fat 6g, Saturated Fat 3g, Total Carbs 5g, Net Carbs 3g, Protein 6g, Sugar 1g, Fiber 2g, salt 0.35g

Lemon Drizzle cake

Prep & cook time: 1 hour 10minutes

Serves: 9

Ingredients

- 200g butter, softened
- 200g golden caster sugar
- 4 eggs
- 175g almond, ground
- 250g mashed potato
- 3 lemon zest
- 2 tbsp baking powder, gluten-free
- For the drizzle
- 4 tbsp granulated sugar
- 1 lemon juice

Directions

1. Preheat oven to 350°F. Line a deep baking tin then grease it with butter.
2. Beat butter and sugar in a mixing bowl until light and fluffy.
3. Gradually beat in the eggs then fold in the ground almonds, potatoes, lemon zest, and baking powder.
4. Tip the mixture into the baking tin, level the top, and bake for 40 minutes or until golden.
5. Turn out the cake on a cooling rack.
6. Mix sugar and lemon juice in a small bowl then spoon over the cake top letting it drip down the sides. Serve and enjoy.

Nutritional Information

Calories 514, Total Fat 36g, Saturated Fat 2g, Total Carbs 41g, Net Carbs 38g, Protein 9g, Sugar 35g, Fiber 2g, salt 0.88g

Orange cake

Prep & cook time: 1 hour 30minutes

Serves: 12

Ingredients

- 18.25 oz yellow cake mix
- 3 oz instant lemon pudding mix
- 3/4 cup orange juice
- 1/2 cup vegetable oil
- 4 eggs
- 1 tbsp lemon extract
- 1/3 cup orange juice
- 2/3 cup white sugar
- 1/4 cup butter

Directions

1. Preheat oven to 350°F.

2. In a mixing bowl, stir together cake mix, and lemon pudding mix. Make a well at the center and pour orange juice, vegetable oil, eggs, lemon extract.

3. Beat until well blended then pour the cake mix into the prepared baking pan.

4. Bake for 50 minutes then transfer the cake to a wire rack.

5. Meanwhile, cook 1/3 cup orange juice, white sugar, and butter in a saucepan for 2 minutes.

6. Drizzle over cake then serve

Nutritional Information: Calories 410, Total Fat 19.8g, Saturated Fat 4.9g, Total Carbs 55g, Net Carbs 54g, Protein 4.2g, Sugar 32g, Fiber 1g.

Rainbow Cake in a Jar

Prep & cook time: 1 hour 20minutes

Serves: 3

Ingredients

- 1 box white cake mix
- Food coloring (yellow, pink. Green, purple, and turquoise)
- 1 can vanilla frosting
- Rainbow sprinkles

Directions

1. Preheat oven to 350°F. Wash the canning jars then dry them.

2. Spray the jars generously with cooking spray.

3. Make the cake mix according to the package directions then divide it into 5 bowls.

4. Add a different food color in each bowl then stir until the color has blended well.

5. Divide each cake mixture among the jars layering the colors in an order.

6. Place the jars in a baking dish then add water to it to surround the jars. Bake for 40 minutes without letting the cakes brown. Allow the cakes to cool then frost and garnish with a rainbow sprinkle. Serve and enjoy.

Nutritional Information: Calories 1330, Total Fat 59g, Saturated Fat 21g, Total Carbs 189g, Net Carbs 180g, Protein 10g, Sugar 124g, Fiber 1g

CHAPTER 6:

Pies Recipes

Cherry Pie

Prep & cook time: 30 minutes

Serves 5

Ingredients:

- One large box of fresh cherries pitted (recommended: several)
- One cup of brown sugar
- One tablespoon of cornstarch
- One teaspoon of cinnamon powder, optional
- One pie crust (or the whole box, frozen)

Directions:

1. Mix Ingredients Sugar and cornstarch in a bowl.
2. Put a layer of cherries into the bottom of the unbaked pie shell. Pour sugar mixture over. Add another layer of cherries, then sugar mixture, and another layer of cherries.
3. Bake for 10 minutes, then turn down to 200F and bake for one hour.
4. Take the pie out of the oven and let cool for 10 minutes more. Add a top crust.
5. Cut slits in the top crust to let out steam.
6. Bake for 10 more minutes.
7. Take the pie out of the oven and eat and enjoy!

Recipe Notes: This pie is best when eaten within the first day it was made.

Note: After the first two days, some of the cherries tend to sink to the bottom of the pie.

Lemon Whipped Cream Pie

Prep & cook time: 50 minutes

Serves 6

Ingredients:

- 1 recipe chocolate cookie dough made with pecans
- 1 -2 tablespoons fresh lemon juice (find one with no bits of lemon skin*)
- 8 tablespoons butter - softened
- 1/4 cup of sugar
- 1 cup heavy cream
- 2 tablespoons vanilla

Directions

1. Soften butter, cream, and sugar. Mix well. Add vanilla. Whip some more. Put the cookie dough into a pie pan and form it to your liking, but make it flat on the bottom.

2. Spread on the butter filling.

3. Make the pie crust for the top of the pie. Put it on top.

4. Whisk the heavy cream until very stiff so you can make mounds with it. Very stiff.

5. Take a spoon full of whipped cream and then place it between the pie and the crust top. Then take another spoon of cream and place it on top of the pie. Then take the spoon and make a design with the whipped cream. Like a wave.

6. Take a knife and remove any pieces of the pie that are on top of the pie, but do not remove too much.

7. Chill for 4 hours and eat

Blueberry Pie

Prep & cook time: 1 hour 15 minutes

Serves 8

Ingredients

- 1 cup of sugar
- 1 teaspoon salt
- 4 cups flour
- 1 or 2 drops of food color (optional)
- 6 tablespoons butter
- 2 egg or egg yolk
- 3 cups fresh blueberries
- tablespoons fresh lemon juice
- 1/3 cup of sugar
- 1 teaspoon vanilla extract

Directions

1. Preheat oven to 425 degrees Fahrenheit

2. Pour the blueberries, lemon juice, and sugar on the stove over medium heat. Cook for about 10 minutes.

3. Combine the flour, sugar, lemon rind, salt, egg, egg yolk, and butter in a bowl. Mix for about a minute to form a coarse dough.

4. Pour the liquid into the dough with a spoon; mix in a circular motion to bring the mixture together. Once a dough forms, cover and let it rest for about 10 minutes in the fridge.

5. Wrap the dough in wax paper and place in the fridge for 45 minutes. After the dough is chilled, roll it out.

6. Place the dough into the pie pan and trim any excess dough.

7. Pour the blueberry mixture into the dough-lined pie pan and add the lemon juice first.

8. Roll out the remaining dough and cover the pie with it. To make the lattice top, cut the remaining dough into strips about ½ inch wide and ½ inch thick. Position a strip diagonally over the pie, remove the top piece, and fold the dough underneath. Place the next strip approximately ¼ inch from the one below and repeat the process until the pie is finished. Brush the dough strips with water and sprinkle sugar on top of the lattice. Bake for 10 minutes more before lowering the temperature to 350 degrees and baking for about 35 minutes more or until the crust turns golden brown. Cool the pie to room temperature.

Oreo Butterscotch Pie

Prep & cook time: 1 hour 10 minutes

Serves 2

Ingredients

- Oreo Pie Crust
- Butterscotch Mousse
- Caramel Ice cream (chocolate ice cream with some butterscotch syrup or something) - Remember it's a light version of caramel butterscotch sauce
- Toppings

Directions

1. Add some milk to the mix and mix it until all the crumbs are mixed well. Put the crumbs into a premade pie crust and spread it on the mixture on the medium heat oven for 20 minutes. After that let it cool down for 20 minutes in the fridge.

2. After that, add the milk to the butterscotch cream and mix it well until it becomes soft. Pour it over the cookie crust and let it stay in the freezer for 20 minutes.

3. Finally, remove the ice cream from the freezer and start making the caramel sauce. Make sure you let it cool down for at least 20 minutes. Add some caramel flakes and a few pieces of cut-up cookies or candies on the other side and put it for 20 minutes again at the freezer.

4. The final touch is to put some whipped cream around the top of the pie. Add some caramel flakes and some cut-up cookies on top of the pie. Serve and enjoy

Strawberry Pie

Prep & cook time: 40 minutes

Serves 4

Ingredients:

- 500g strawberries
- 400g sugar
- 4g salt
- 2g lemon juice
- 4g baking powder
- 2g erythritol
- 1 0g corn starch
- 3g sodium alginate
- 3g guar gum

- 1 batter: 135g
- 2 eggs
- 135g oil
- 135g flour
- 45g cream, 1 recipe pie crust

Directions

1. Peel & Slice strawberries into 1.5cm pieces. Dissolve sodium alginate in 10g water & 1g salt, then add into 60g water. Combine strawberries & sodium alginate solution.
2. Dissolve corn starch into 120g water, and add into 60g water. Make pie crust, pour into pie mold, let crust cool down. Prepare cream, combine cream with gelatin, mix until no lumps remain.
3. Cook strawberry & corn starch solution in a sauce pan, add in cream & gelatin mix. Add in remaining Ingredients, return to medium heat and stir until thickened. Scoop strawberry & cream mixture into pie crust.
4. Bake at 180°C for 10 minutes. Remove from oven, and chill in the refrigerator for 24 hours.

Apple Pie

Prep & cook time: 50 minutes
Serves 2

Ingredients:
- Apples
- Soft butter
- Flour Sugar
- Cinnamon

Directions:

1. Cut apples; take out the seeds; mix the dry Ingredients; mash the apple chunks; add the dry Ingredients slowly as to not turn the dough into a blob of sugar and flour; make sure that the apple chunks are spread through the dough; add milk slowly to the dough; make sure that. the dough is still thick enough to fit on the pie dish; throw the dough onto the floured surface; form it into two disks; put on a buttered pie dish; cut decorative shapes into the pie crust;
2. Cook at 400 degrees for 30-45 minutes; make sure there is some burning before you take it out; turn onto a cooling rack; enjoy.

CHAPTER 7:

Snacks and Desserts Recipes

Cheddar Biscuits

Prep & cook time: 45 minutes

Serves: 10

Ingredients:

- 2 cups of biscuit mix
- A quarter cup of butter
- ⅔ of a cup of milk
- A single cup of mild cheddar cheese that is shredded
- A quarter teaspoon of garlic powder

Directions:

1. Heat your oven to 450 F.
2. Grease a baking sheet.
3. Mix the biscuit mix, milk, and cheese in a bowl. Make sure that the batter is doughy and soft. A wooden spoon will help with this, and it should take half a minute.
4. Put the batter on the sheet in spoonfuls.
5. Bake 10 minutes, and the biscuits should be a light brown.
6. Heat the garlic and butter in a pan on low heat until it is melted. This will take 5 minutes.
7. Brush that mix over the biscuits.

This recipe will take 20 minutes to complete.

Nutritional information (per serving): Calories-385 Fat-24.6 grams Carbs-31.5 grams Protein-10.2 grams

Lemon Raspberry Muffins

Prep & cook time: 60 minutes

Serves 12

Ingredients:

- Half a cup of honey
- 2 eggs
- A single cup of plain Greek yogurt
- A single cup and ¾ of white whole wheat flour
- A single teaspoon of baking powder
- Half a teaspoon of baking soda
- A third of a cup of coconut oil that is melted
- 2 teaspoons of vanilla extract
- The zest from a lemon
- A single cup and a half of organic raspberries
- A single tablespoon of turbinado sugar

Directions:

1. Heat your oven to 350 F.
2. Grease a 12 cup muffin tin with coconut oil or cooking spray.
3. Get a large bowl. Combine flour, baking soda, baking powder, and blend with a whisk. Get another bowl and combine the honey oil, and beat them together with a whisk.
4. Add in the eggs and beat them well before adding the zest, vanilla, and yogurt. Mix it all well. If the oil gets solid, microwave it for half a minute. Pour your wet Ingredients into the dry. Mix it with a large spoon until it has just combined.
5. Fold raspberries in the batter. It will be thick. Divided into 12 cups and add sugar to the top. Bake 24 minutes and the toothpick should come out clean.
6. Let cool on a cooling rack.

Nutritional information (per serving): Calories-193 Fat-7.5 grams Carbs-28.7 grams Protein-5.3 grams

Blueberry Pound Cake

Prep & cook time: 1 hour 30 minutes

Serves 10

Ingredients:

- 2 Tablespoons of butter
- A quarter cup of white sugar
- 2 ¾ cups of all-purpose flour
- A single teaspoon of baking powder
- A single cup of butter
- 4 eggs
- 2 cups of white sugar
- 2 cups of blueberries that are fresh
- A single teaspoon of vanilla extract
- A quarter cup of flour that is all-purpose

Directions:

1. Preheat your oven to 325 F. Grease a pan that is 10 inches with 2 tablespoons of butter.
2. Sprinkle that same pan with a quarter cup of sugar. Mix 2 ¾ of the cup of flour with the baking powder and place it to the side.
3. Get a bowl and cream a cup of butter and 2 cups of sugar together until it has become fluffy and light. Beat the eggs one at a time before stirring the vanilla in. Slowly beat in your flour mix. Dredge your berries with the last quarter cup of flour.
4. Fold into the batter before pouring it into your prepared pan. Bake for 80 minutes. The toothpick test should show a clean toothpick.
5. Let cool for 10 minutes into the pan before letting it cool on a wire rack.

Nutritional information (per serving): Calories-338 Fat-14.5 grams Carbs-48.8 grams Protein-4.3 grams

Pizza Pockets

Prep & cook time: 40 minutes

Serves 4

Ingredients:

- A third of a cup of Parmesan that is grated
- A quarter of a cup of Parmesan that is grated

- 8 ounces of turkey sausage (Italian)
- A single tablespoon of olive oil
- A single beaten egg
- A single cup and a half of marinara sauce
- All-purpose flour
- A single pizza crust store-bought
- 4 ounces of room temperature cream cheese
- A cup of arugula tightly packed

Directions:

1. Heat your olive oil over a heat that is medium-high and in a medium heavy skillet.
2. Add in the sausage and cook until it is golden and crumbled. 5 minutes. Add the arugula and cook it until it has wilted. Turn off your heat and let it cool for 19 minutes. Add in your cream cheese and a third of the parmesan. Stir, so it combines.
3. Preheat your oven to 400 F. Roll out your dough and make a big rectangle. Cut it in half.
4. Do this again until you have eight equal rectangles. Put your toppings onto one of the sides of each rectangle. Brush the edges with egg wash. Close the rectangle of dough over the topping. Use a fork to seal them up.
5. Put the pockets on the baking sheet that is lined with parchment paper. Brush the tops with egg wash. Sprinkle the rest of the cheese on top. Bake for 15 minutes. Heat your marinara sauce over low heat. Serve with sauce when done.

Nutritional information (per serving): Calories-385 Fat- 19 grams Carbs-37 grams Protein-17 grams Fiber-1.5 grams

Croissants

Prep & cook time: 60 minutes

Serves 12

Ingredients:

- A single cup of milk
- 4 cups of flour that is all-purpose
- A third of a cup of sugar that is granulated
- 2 and a quarter teaspoon of salt that is kosher
- 4 teaspoons of yeast that is active and dry
- A cup and a quarter of butter that is cold and unsalted
- An egg wash (this is to have a single large egg, and you beat it with a teaspoon of water)

Directions:

1. Place your yeast and salt along with the flour and sugar in a bowl and whisk it all together until it has combined well. Slice your butter into slices an eighth of an inch thick and toss it into the flour mix so that the butter is coated.
2. Add your milk in and stir it together. A stiff dough will be made. Wrap your dough and make sure it's tight. You are going to use plastic wrap. Let it chill for 60 minutes.
3. Get yourself a lightly floured surface and roll your dough into a big and long rectangle.

4. Fold and make it like a letter. This means you fold it into thirds. Turn it 90 degrees and repeat 4 times. The dough should be flat and smooth with streaks of butter in it.

5. Rewrap it again and chill for another 60 minutes. Divide the dough in half and then roll again. It should be an eighth of an inch thick. Cut your dough into triangles that are long and skinny. Notch your wide end of each triangle you made with a half-inch cut.

6. Roll from the wide end to the end with a point. Tuck the point under the croissant.

7. Place on a baking sheet that is lined with parchment. Cover with plastic wrap (loosely) and allow it to proof for 120 minutes. Preheat your oven to 375 F. Brush the croissants with your egg wash. Bake 20 minutes. They should be a puffy brown golden color, and they should be flaky.

Nutritional information (per serving): Calories-294 Fat-16 grams Protein- 5 grams Fiber- 1 gram Carbs- 31 grams

Almond-Raisin Granola

Prep & cook time: 1 hour 45 minutes

Serves 5

Ingredients:

- Half a cup of flax seeds
- Half a cup of sunflower seed kernels
- A cup of raw almonds that are sliced
- 3 cups of oats that are old-fashioned
- A quarter cup of melted coconut oil
- A single cup of raisins
- 6 tablespoons of honey
- 6 tablespoons of pure maple syrup
- 2 tablespoons of water that is warm

Directions:

1. Heat your oven to 250 and line a jelly roll pan with baking parchment.

2. Mix everything but the water, oil, honey, and syrup in a bowl and whisk the water, oil, honey, and syrup in another bowl. Make sure that the honey mix is smooth.

3. Pour the oat mix bowl into the honey bowl. Spread the mix on the pan in a layer that is even. Bake for an hour but up to an hour and a half until the color is a golden brown.

4. Take out of the oven and make sure that you let it cool completely. Take the granola off by lifting the paper. Break it and place in a bowl adding your choice of Ingredients and then mix it.

5. Store in an airtight container.

Nutritional information (per serving): Calories-568 Protein-12.4 grams Fat-27.2 grams Carbs0-76.4 grams

Jam Pockets

Prep & cook time: 2 hours 20 minutes

Serves 15

Ingredients:

- A single teaspoon of vanilla
- A single egg
- 2 cups of flour
- Half a cup of powdered sugar

- A single cup of butter that is cut into cubes and cold

Directions:

1. Preheat your oven to 375. Use a food processor and combine your sugar and flour until they have mixed.
2. Toss in your butter and give it a few long buzzes with it until it has a cornmeal look.
3. Add the vanilla and egg and then buzz it twice more. You should be left with a soft dough. Cover with plastic wrap and then let it chill in the fridge for a couple of hours.
4. Roll out our dough and use a cookie cutter to make circles.
5. Add the jam of your choice to the center and fold your edges inward. It should overlap in the middle. Bake 10 minutes. The bottom should be a faint brown color.
6. When cooled, sprinkle sugar over the top.

Banana Bread

Prep & cook time: 1 hour 10 minutes

Serves 12

Ingredients:

- A single teaspoon of baking soda
- ¾ of a cup of sugar
- Half a cup of pecans that have been chopped
- 3 bananas medium in size and mashed
- Half a cup of mayonnaise
- A single egg
- A cup and a half of flour

Directions:

1. Preheat your oven to 350. Get a bowl. Mix the egg, mayonnaise, and bananas. Get another bowl.
2. Mix the baking soda, pecans, flour, and sugar in the bowl. Add the flour mix to the wet mix and stir until combined.
3. The mix will be very thick; this is alright. If you over-mix, it won't be right.
4. Grease a pan. Pour the mix into the pan and bake for an hour. A toothpick should come out clean.
5. Remove from the pan and make sure it cools completely.

Nutritional information (per serving): Calories-231 Fat-10 grams Fiber- 1 gram Protein-2 grams

Carbs-31 grams

Cranberry Ice-Cream Pie

Prep & cook Time: 35 minutes

Servings: 8

Ingredients:

- 2 tbsp. sliced almonds, toasted
- 2 cups whipped topping
- 1 tbsp. orange juice
- 1 cup whole-berry cranberry sauce, canned
- 2 cups vanilla ice cream, softened
- 9-inch chocolate crumb pie shell

Directions:

1. Place the pie shell in the freezer to chill while making the filling.
2. In a bowl, combine orange juice, cranberry sauce, and ice cream and stir with a spoon to blend well.
3. Spoon the ice cream mixture into the chilled shell and continue freezing for another 4 hours, or until the pie is firm. Spread the topping over the shell before sprinkling with almonds. Cover and place in the freezer again for about 30 minutes, remove and allow the pie to stand for 20 minutes before serving.

Nutrition: Calories: 359kcal Fat: 16g Cholesterol: 40mg Sodium: 312mg Carbohydrate: 52g

Protein: 3g

Cookie Dough Bites

Prep& cook Time: 1 hour 20 minutes

Servings: 6

Ingredients:

- 6 ounces small chocolate chips
- 2 cups flour
- 1 tsp. vanilla extract
- 1 1/2 cups light brown sugar
- 1 cup salted butter, softened

Directions:

1. Combine sugar and butter in a bowl.
2. Add all the remaining Ingredients and mix well –using your hands will mix the Ingredients better.
3. Roll the mixture into 1-inch balls.
4. Place the balls in the refrigerator for about 30 minutes. Drizzle the balls with chocolate, dip in chocolate or eat as is –whichever way, they are equally delicious!
5. Before serving, allow the balls to stand at room temperature for about 10 minutes.
6. Refrigerate the remains.

Nutrition: Total Fat 2.3 g Saturated Fat 1.3 g Unsaturated Fat 0.5 g Cholesterol 3.9 mg Sodium 42.5 mg Total Carbohydrate 32.6 g Protein 1.6 g

Surprise Pie

Prep & cook Time: 10 minutes

Servings: 1

Ingredients:

- Fat-free or low-fat chocolate pudding
- Whipped cream
- 1 jar peanut butter
- 2-3 Cups Rice Krispies cereal

Directions:

1. Place some rice crispies into a medium bowl, add some peanut butter, and mix until well blended. Place the mixture into an empty crust pan and push it firmly to the pan.
2. Sprinkle the whipped cream on top of the Rice Krispies mixture.
3. Prepare the pudding and add on top of the whipped cream.

4. Leave in the refrigerator for half an hour before serving.

Nutrition: Calories: 623 kcal Fat: 36.2g Carbohydrates: 69g Protein: 10.5g Cholesterol: 43mg

Sodium: 394mg

Easy Fudge

Prep& cook Time: 15 minutes

Servings: 16 pieces

Ingredients:

- 1 can sweetened condensed milk
- 1 stick butter
- 3 C. flavored chips (chocolate, butterscotch or white chocolate)

Directions:

1. Place all the Ingredients in a microwave bowl and microwave for about 4 minutes, stirring until all Ingredients are melted.
2. Grease a 9x9-inch pan with cooking spray. Add other Ingredients such as coconut, raisins, or any other nuts if desired. Leave in the refrigerator for about four hours to set.
3. Cut into squares and serve immediately!

Nutrition: Calories: 90.6 Total Fat: 3.5g Cholesterol: 5mg Sodium: 17mg Potassium: 29.4mg

Carbohydrates: 14.3g Protein: 0.5g

Apple Cake

Prep & cook Time: 1 hour 35 minutes

Servings: 6

Ingredients:

Topping:

- ½ cup brown sugar (packed)
- ½ teaspoon cinnamon
- ½ cup chocolate chips (or chopped walnuts)

Base:

- 3 tablespoons margarine
- ⅓ cup apple sauce
- ½ cup of sugar
- ½ cup brown sugar (packed)
- 1 egg
- ½ teaspoon baking soda
- ½ cup milk
- 1 teaspoon baking powder
- ¼ teaspoon cinnamon
- 1 ½ cup flour
- 1 teaspoon vanilla
- 2 large apples, peeled (cored and chopped)
- chocolate chips (optional)

Directions:

1. Mix margarine, applesauce, sugars, and egg. In a small bowl, dissolve baking soda in milk. Add to sugar mixture. Add baking powder, spices, and flour.
2. Mix just until flour disappears. Add apples and a spoonful of chocolate chips (add as

much as you like). Pour batter into a sprayed baking pan.

3. Sprinkle with topping.
4. Bake at 350 F for 40-45 minutes.

Nutrition: Calories: 490kcal Total Fat: 25g Cholesterol: 115mg Sodium: 380mg Potassium: 230mg Total Carbohydrate: 60g Protein: 7g

Key Lime Pie

Prep & cook Time: 50 minutes

Servings: 6 - 8

Ingredients:

Crust:

- 1 ½ cup chocolate wafers or Oreo cookie crumbs
- 3 tablespoons of melted margarine

Filling:

- 2 eggs
- 4 egg yolks
- 2 tbsp grated lime zest
- 3 cans nonfat sweetened condensed milk
- 1 cup lime juice (4 to 6 limes)
- green food coloring (optional)
- ¼ cup whipping cream

Directions:

1. Preheat the oven to 350 degrees F. Bake the crust for 8-10 minutes.
2. Let cool at room temperature for about 20 minutes. In a mixer bowl, place the eggs, egg yolks, and zest. Beat on low speed for 2 minutes. Beat in the condensed milk and then the lime juice.
3. If you are unhappy with the color, add a couple of drops of green food coloring.
4. Pour the lime filling into the crust. Bake at 325 F for approximately 20 minutes until the center is set. Let cool and refrigerate for at least 3 hours until well chilled.
5. The pies can be covered with an oil-sprayed plastic wrap. For garnish, add the whipping cream.

Nutrition: Calories: 440kcal Total Fat: 22g Cholesterol: 146mg Sodium: 206mg Potassium: 327mg Total Carbohydrates: 54g Protein: 8.4g

Lemon Squares

Prep & cook Time: 2 hours

Servings: 25

Ingredients:

- 1 cup all-purpose flour
- ¼ cup of sugar
- ¼ cup margarine
- 2 tablespoons yogurt

For the topping:

- ¾ cup of sugar
- 2 tablespoons flour
- ½ teaspoon baking powder
- ¼ teaspoon salt
- 1 egg

- 1 egg white
- 1 lemon (zest)
- ¼ cup lemon juice
- 2 teaspoons icing sugar

Directions:

1. In a bowl, mix flour, sugar, margarine, and yogurt until combined.
2. Press into an 8-inch square pan lightly coated with cooking spray. Bake in a preheated oven at 325 F for 10 minutes.
3. For the topping, combine sugar, flour, baking powder, salt, egg, egg white, lemon zest, and juice and mix well.
4. Pour over base and bake for 20 minutes until the top is set.
5. Let cool in the pan. Sift icing sugar on top before cutting into squares.

Nutrition: Total Fat: 4g Cholesterol: 25mg Sodium: 70g Potassium: 15mg Total Carbohydrate: 13g Protein 1g

Honey Pear Crisp

Prep & cook Time: 20 minutes

Servings: 6

Ingredients:

- ½ cup uncooked old-fashioned oats
- ¼ all-purpose flour
- ⅓ cup packed light brown sugar
- ¼ teaspoon cinnamon
- ¼ teaspoon nutmeg
- ⅛ teaspoon salt
- ¼ cup (½ stick) butter (softened)
- 4 peeled pears (halved and cored)
- 1 tablespoon lemon juice
- 2 tablespoons honey
- whipped cream or vanilla ice cream (optional)

Directions:

1. Preheat the oven to 375 degrees F.
2. Coat a 9-inch pie plate with nonstick cooking spray.
3. In a medium bowl stir together the oats, flour, brown sugar, cinnamon, nutmeg, and salt until well mixed.
4. With your fingers, work in the butter until a crumbly mixture forms.
5. Place the pears in the pie plate cut side up.
6. Sprinkle the pears with lemon juice and drizzle with honey.
7. Crumble the oat topping all over the pears.
8. Bake until pears are softened and the topping is crisp and lightly browned. That should take about 25 minutes. Let stand for 15 minutes.
9. Serve with whipped cream or ice cream if you like.

Nutrition: Calories: 291kcal Total Fat: 11.9g Cholesterol: 20.4mg Sodium: 129.3mg

Total Carbohydrates: 46.4g Protein: 3.5g

Frozen Fruit Bites

Prep & cook Time: 1 hour 10 minutes

Servings: 12

Ingredients:

- 1 tsp. lemon juice
- 1/2 cup cream cheese, softened
- 1/2 cup vanilla yogurt
- 12 vanilla wafer cookies
- 1 tsp. honey
- Sliced strawberries, kiwi, or whole blueberries

Directions:

1. Line a mini-cupcake pan with liners. Place a wafer cookie, flat side up, on each well's bottom.
2. Whisk together honey, lemon juice, cream cheese, and yogurt in a medium bowl until smooth. Using a spoon, scoop one heaping on top of each wafer cookie, and top each with the fruit.
3. Using a plastic wrap, cover the pan and place it in the freezer for about 1 ½ hour, or until the fruit bites are firm; remove, wait for about 25 minutes and serve.

Nutrition: Calories: 63kcal Total Fat: 4g Protein: 1g

Honey Milk Balls

Prep & cook Time: 10 minutes

Servings: 20

Ingredients:

- 1 cup rolled oats
- 1 cup powdered milk
- 1/2 cup honey
- 1/2 cup peanut butter

Directions:

1. Mix all the Ingredients, roll into small balls, and refrigerate for about 60 minutes.
2. You can eat the balls plain, dipped in chocolate, or rolled in powdered sugar.

Nutrition: Calories: 45kcal Fat: 1.5g Sodium: 35mg Potassium: 94mg Carbohydrates: 6g

Protein: 2g

Banana Bread Cobbler

Prep & cook Time: 60 Minutes

Servings: 6

Ingredients:

- cup rolled oats
- 3/4 cup brown sugar
- 1/2 cup flour
- 1/2 cup vegan margarine, softened
- Cobbler
- cup flour
- 2/3 Cup of sugar
- 1/2 teaspoons baking powder
- 1/2 teaspoon salt
- cup non-dairy milk
- 1/2 cup vegan margarine, melted

- ripe bananas, sliced

Directions:

1. Preheat the oven to 375 degrees. Lightly grease an 8-inch square pan.

2. To top up the sesame oil: In a medium bowl, whisk together the oats, sugar, flour, and margarine until crushed.

3. To make the cobbler, in a large bowl, beat the flour, sugar, baking powder, and salt until combined.

4. Add the non-dairy milk and melted margarine until combined. Pour the batter into the pan and place the banana slices on top.

5. Cover the plants with the steel cover and bake until golden brown, about 40 minutes, or until a toothpick inserted in the center comes out clean and with a few crumbs.

6. Serve hot or at room temperature with a spoonful of vanilla ice cream, if desired.

NUTRITION: Calorie: 490 kcal Fat: 24 g Carbs: 68 g Sodium: 420 mg Protein: 5 g

Yummy Chocolate Cake

Prep & cook Time: 55 Minutes

Servings: 16

Ingredients:

- package chocolate cake mix (regular size)
- package (2.1 oz.) sugar-free instant chocolate pudding mix
- 1-3/4 cups water
- egg whites

Frosting:

- 1-1/4 cups cold fat-free milk
- 1/4 teaspoon almond extract
- package (1.4 oz.) sugar-free instant chocolate pudding mix
- carton (8 oz.) frozen reduced-fat whipped topping, thawed
- Chocolate curls, optional

Directions:

1. Blend egg whites, water, pudding mix, and cake mix in a big bowl.

2. Beat for 60 seconds over low speed, then switch to medium speed and beat for 2 minutes.

3. Transfer to a 15x10x1-inch baking pan greased with cooking spray.

4. Bake at 350 degrees until a toothpick slid into the middle comes out with no streaks of batter, about 12 to 18 minutes. Allow cooling on a wire rack.

5. Put extract and milk into a big bowl to make the frosting. Scatter in 1/3 of the pudding mix and allow to stand for 60 seconds.

6. Stir pudding into milk. Do the same thing two times with the rest of the pudding mix. Stir pudding for another 2 minutes.

7. Allow sitting for 15 minutes. Fold whipped topping into the mixture.

8. Frost the cake. If preferred, add on chocolate curls to decorate.

NUTRITION: Calories: 197 Carbohydrate: 35 g Fat: 5 g Protein: 3 g Sodium: 409 mg

Walnut-coconut Coffee Cake

Preparation Time: 1 hour 10 Minutes

Servings: 12-15

Ingredients:

- 1 cup of vegetable oil
- 1 cup of sugar
- 1 cup of packed brown sugar
- 2 large eggs
- 1 teaspoon vanilla extract
- 2-1/2 cups all-purpose flour
- 1 teaspoon baking soda
- A pinch teaspoon salt
- 1 teaspoon ground cinnamon
- 1 cup buttermilk
- 1 cup sweetened shredded coconut
- 1 cup chopped walnuts
- Confectioners' sugar, optional

Directions:

1. Mix the vanilla, eggs, sugars, and oil well in a big bowl.
2. Mix cinnamon, salt, baking soda, and flour; put to egg mixture alternating with buttermilk. Mix till just moisten.
3. Mix in walnuts and coconut till just combined.
4. Put in a 13x9-inch greased baking pan; bake for 45-55 minutes at 350° till an inserted toothpick in middle exits clean; cool down on a wire rack.
5. If desired, dust using confectioners' sugar.

NUTRITION: Calories: 410 Carbohydrate: 48 g Fat: 22 g Protein: 6 g Sodium: 289 mg

Raspberry Supreme Cheesecake

Prep & cook Time: 50 Minutes

Servings: 16-20

Ingredients:

- 2 cups graham cracker crumbs
- 1 cup chopped toasted almonds
- 1/2 cup of sugar
- 2/3 cup butter, melted
- package (8 oz.) cream cheese softened
- can (14 oz.) sweetened condensed milk
- 1/3 cup lemon juice
- teaspoon vanilla extract
- package (6 oz.) raspberry gelatin
- cups hot water
- packages (10 oz. each) frozen raspberries, partially thawed
- cups whipped cream
- 1/4 cup toasted slivered almonds

Direction:

1. Mix the first 4 Ingredients. Press into a 13x9-inch dish; chill for half an hour.
2. In the meantime, whisk vanilla, lemon juice, milk, and cream cheese until smooth. Pour over the crust; chill.
3. Dissolve the gelatin in the water. Add the raspberries, stir until they are thawed completely; chill until they become very thick.
4. Pour over the fillings. Chill until set. Add almonds and whipped cream on top before serving.
5. Chill in the fridge.

NUTRITION: Calories: 313 Carbohydrate: 43 g Fat: 14 g Protein: 5 g Sodium: 178 mg

White Chocolate Torte

Prep & cook Time: 1 hour 10 Minutes

Servings: 14-16

Ingredients:

1 cup butter, softened

2 cups sugar

4 oz. white baking chocolate, melted and cooled

4 large eggs

1-1/2 teaspoons clear vanilla extract

3 cups all-purpose flour

1 teaspoon baking soda

1 cup buttermilk

1/2 cup water

1/2 cup chopped pecans, toasted

Frosting:

- 11 oz. cream cheese, softened
- 1/3 cup butter, softened
- 4 oz. white baking chocolate, melted and cooled
- 1-1/2 teaspoons clear vanilla extract
- 6-1/2 cups confectioners' sugar
- Chocolate curls

Directions:

1. Line waxed paper on 3 9-in. greased round baking pans; grease paper. Put aside.
2. Combine sugar and butter and cream till fluffy and light in a big bowl; beat chocolate in. One by one, add eggs; beat well with every addition.
3. Beat vanilla in. Mix baking soda and flour; alternately with water and buttermilk, add to the creamed mixture slowly.
4. Beat well with every addition. Fold pecans in; put the batter in prepped pans.
5. Bake for 23-27 minutes at 350 degrees F or till inserted toothpick in middle exits clean; cool for 10 minutes.
6. Transfer from pans onto wire racks. Throw waxed paper.
7. Frosting: Beat cream cheese and butter till fluffy in a big bowl; beat vanilla and chocolate in.
8. Add confectioners' sugar slowly till smooth; spread frosting on top, sides, and between layers of cake.

9. Garnish using chocolate curls; keep in the fridge.

NUTRITION: Calories: 885 Carbohydrate: 103 g Fat: 49 g Protein: 11 g Sodium: 491 mg

Raspberry Swirl Cheesecake Pie

Prep & cook Time: 55 Minutes

Servings: 6-8

Ingredients:

- Pastry for single-crust pie (9 inches)
- 2 packages (8 oz. each) cream cheese, softened
- 1/2 cup of sugar
- 1/2 teaspoon vanilla extract
- 2 eggs
- 3 tablespoons raspberry jam

Direction:

1. Use heavy-duty foil with double thickness to line unpicked pastry shell. Bake for 5 minutes at 450 degrees; take away the foil.
2. Bake for another 5 minutes. Take out of the oven, lower the temperature to 350 degrees.
3. Whisk vanilla, sugar, and cream cheese together in a bowl. Add eggs, whisking on low speed until just blended.
4. Add to the pastry shell. Whisk jam, drizzle the jam over the filling. Swirl the jam by slicing through the filling with a knife.
5. Bake until the middle has nearly set, about 25-30 minutes. Place on a wire rack to cool, about 60 minutes.

6. Chill overnight. Allow sitting at room temperature before cutting, about 30 minutes.

NUTRITION: Calories: 305 Carbohydrate: 31 g Fat: 18 g Protein: 5 g Sodium: 200 mg

Cherry Cheese Delight

Preparation Time: 1 hour

Servings: 12-15

Ingredients:

1 cup all-purpose flour

1 cup chopped pecans

1/2 cup packed brown sugar

1/2 cup butter, softened

Filling:

- 2 packages (8 oz. each) cream cheese, softened
- 1/2 cup confectioners' sugar
- 1 teaspoon vanilla extract
- carton (12 oz.) frozen whipped topping
- cans (21 oz. each) cherry pie filling

Directions:

1. Mix the brown sugar, pecans, and flour in a small bowl. Mix in the butter till crumbly.
2. Pat lightly into a 13x9-inch ungreased baking dish. Bake for 18 to 20 minutes at 350 degrees, until golden brown.
3. Cool entirely. Beat the vanilla, confectioner's sugar, and cream cheese until smooth in a large bowl for the filling.

4. Fold in the whipped topping. Spread the filling over the crust carefully.
5. Add pie filling on top. Cover then put in the fridge for a minimum of 2 hours.

NUTRITION: Calories: 344 Carbohydrate: 35 g Fat: 21 g Protein: 3 g Sodium: 117 mg

Zucchini Chip Cupcakes

Preparation Time: 50 minutes

Servings: 2 dozen.

Ingredients:

1/2 cup butter, softened

1/2 cup canola oil

1-3/4 cups sugar

2 eggs

1/2 cup milk

1 teaspoon vanilla extract

2-1/2 cups all-purpose flour

1/4 cup baking cocoa

1 teaspoon baking soda

1/2 teaspoon salt

1/2 teaspoon ground cinnamon

2 cups shredded zucchini

1/4 cup miniature semisweet chocolate chips

1/4 cup chopped pecans

Directions:

1. Cream sugar, oil, and butter in a large bowl until they are fluffy and light. Whisk in vanilla, milk, and eggs.
2. Mix cinnamon, salt, baking soda, cocoa, and flour; add into the creamed mixture gradually Fold in chocolate chips and zucchini.
3. Add into paper-lined or greased muffin cups to 2/3 full. Place pecans on top.
4. Bake at 375 degrees until a toothpick comes out clean, for 20-25 minutes.
5. Let cool for 10 minutes, then transfer from the pans onto wire racks to cool entirely

NUTRITION: Calories: 208 Carbohydrate: 27 g Fat: 11 g Protein: 3 g Sodium: 149 mg

Cinnamon Cupcakes

Prep & cook Time: 1 hour 25 Minutes

Servings: 18

Ingredients:

3/4 cup butter, softened

1-1/4 cups sugar

4 large egg whites

1 teaspoon vanilla extract

2-1/4 cups cake flour

2 teaspoons baking powder

1/2 teaspoon salt

Cinnamon frosting:

1/4 cup butter, softened

1 teaspoon clear vanilla extract

1/4 teaspoon ground cinnamon

2-1/4 cups confectioners' sugar

3 tablespoons. 2 percent milk

Additional ground cinnamon

3/4 cup 2 percent milk

Topping:

2 tablespoons sugar

1/2 teaspoon ground cinnamon

Directions:

1. Add sugar and butter, the cream till fluffy and light in a small bowl; beat in vanilla and egg whites.
2. Mix salt, flour, and baking powder; alternately with milk, add to the creamed mixture slowly, beating well after each.
3. Fill the paper-lined muffin cups to 2/3 full. Mix cinnamon and sugar; sprinkle 1/4 teaspoon. on each cupcake.
4. Bake for 16-18 minutes at 375 degrees till inserted toothpick in middle exits clean; cool it for 10 minutes.
5. Transfer from pans onto wire racks; fully cool. Frosting: Cream cinnamon, vanilla, and butter in a small bowl; beat in confectioners' sugar slowly.
6. Add milk; beat till fluffy and light. Frost cupcakes; sprinkle extra cinnamon.

NUTRITION: Calories: 280 kcal Carbohydrate: 44 g Fat: 11 g Protein: 3 g Sodium: 201 mg

Chapter 8:

Frosting Recipes

Vanilla Buttercream Frosting

Prep & cook time: 15 minutes

Serves 6

Ingredients

- ½ pound unsalted butter softened
- cup meringue powder
- 2½-3 cups confectioners' sugar
- teaspoons vanilla extract (preferably pure)
- 10-12 tablespoons milk or heavy cream
- tablespoon pure vanilla extract (optional)

Directions

1. Combine the butter, cream, and sugar in the bowl of a stand mixer fitted with a paddle attachment. If you don't have a mixer, you can use a hand-held electric mixer using the same mixing technique described above.

2. Cream on medium speed until smooth and creamy, 2-4 minutes. Add the vanilla extract and beat 1 minute more. Add the meringue powder and beat 2 minutes, pausing to scrape down the sides of the bowl if needed. With the mixer on low speed, add ½ cup milk and mix just until smooth. If you need more milk to reach a spreading consistency, alternate adding small amounts of milk with a tablespoon or two of meringue powder at a time until you reach your desired consistency. If necessary, add additional sugar or milk to adjust sweetness. If you'd like to add a slight vanilla bean flavor and color, add the 1 tablespoon of vanilla extract with the last addition of milk.

3. Use immediately or chill for 1 hour in the refrigerator. To keep a frosted cake fresh longer, after frosting the cake, cover it with a layer of plastic wrap that has been coated with nonstick cooking spray before you put the top layer of cake on. Unless your plastic wrap is coated with nonstick cooking spray, your cake will become soggy when covered with frosting from condensation from the top layer of the cake.

4. Cover cakes with a layer of plastic wrap directly on the frosting is an easy way to avoid this problem.

Hot Chocolate Whipped Cream Cake

Prep & cook time: 1 hour

Serves 12

Ingredients:

- Cake: 10 tablespoons (1 1/4 sticks) butter softened

- 2 cups sugar
- 2 large eggs
- cup all-purpose flour
- teaspoons baking powder
- 1/2 teaspoon salt
- 3/4 cup whole milk Whipped Cream

Topping:

- 3 cups heavy whipping cream
- 1/2 cup of sugar
- 1 teaspoon vanilla extract

Chocolate Glaze:

- 6 ounces' semisweet chocolate chopped
- ounce unsweetened chocolate chopped 2 tablespoons.

Directions

1. . Mix flour, baking powder, and salt in a bowl. Cream the butter and sugar until light and fluffy in a large mixing bowl. Add eggs one at a time, beating well after each addition.
2. Combine milk and dry Ingredients; add to creamed mixture alternately with milk, beginning and ending with dry Ingredients.3. Beat cake batter at medium speed for 1 minute.
3. Line three 8- or 9-inch round cake pans with waxed paper or parchment paper, and grease and flour bottoms and sides of pans.4. Divide batter among prepared pans; smooth tops with spatula.5. Bake at 350 degrees for 25 to 30 minutes, until a wooden pick inserted in the center comes out clean. Cool 10 minutes in pans; remove to wire racks to cool completely.
4. Bake at 350 degrees for 25 to 30 minutes, until a wooden pick inserted in the center comes out clean. Cool 10 minutes in pans; remove to wire racks to cool completely.
5. To make the whipped cream topping: Combine heavy cream, sugar, and vanilla extract in a bowl; beat with an electric mixer on low speed until soft peaks form (tips curl).
6. To assemble the cake: Place one cake layer on a serving platter. Spread 1 cup whipped cream over top, and sprinkle with 1/4 cup cocoa. Repeat for the second layer. Top with the third layer, and spread remaining whipped cream on top of the cake, swirling lightly with a knife to create a marbled effect.
7. To make the glaze: Combine chocolates in a 3-quart saucepan. Heat and stir over medium heat until melted and smooth, about 8 minutes. Remove from heat; let cool 10 minutes. While chocolate is still warm, pour over whipped cream layer on the cake. Using a spatula, spread evenly to the edges of the cake. Refrigerate at least 1 hour before serving.

Cream Cheese Frosting

Prep & cook time: 10 minutes

Serves 2

Ingredients:

- Cream cheese softened
- 3½ cups powdered sugar
- 2 teaspoons vanilla extract

2 cup (1 stick) butter, softened

2 tablespoons water, milk, or cream

- teaspoon clear vanilla extract (optional)

Direction:

1. Combine all Ingredients in a large mixing bowl.
2. Beat at low speed for 3 minutes, scraping the sides of the bowl.
3. Increase to medium speed and beat for 2 minutes longer, scraping the sides of the bowl as necessary. Use immediately or cover and chill overnight.

Chocolate Frosting

Prep & cook time: 15 minutes

Serves 10

Ingredients

- A cup of butter
- 4 cups sifted confectioners' sugar
- teaspoons vanilla
- 1/4 cup cocoa powder

Directions

1. Cream together butter and sugar until light and fluffy.
2. Add vanilla and cocoa powder; mix well.
3. Refrigerate leftovers for up to a week, but bring frosting back to room temperature before using again.

Peanut Butter Frosting

Prep & cook time: 30 minutes

Serves 5

Ingredients:

- A cup of butter
- 2 pounds' confectioner's sugar sifted
- 2 cups crunchy peanut butter
- 2 teaspoons vanilla extract
- 1-1/2 cups chopped 85% dark chocolate (or use milk chocolate)
- 1/2 cup milk

Directions:

1. Preheat oven to 350 degrees F.
2. Grease and flour three 8-inch round cake pans. Then, sift the sugar and set it aside for later use. Melt the butter over low heat in a saucepan, and then add the peanut butter and vanilla.
3. Once the mixture is smooth, stir in chocolate until melted; set aside to cool for 10 minutes.

Vanilla Cloud Frosting

Prep & cook time: 20 minutes

Serves 10

Ingredients:

- 2 cups of butter or margarine, softened (1 cup = 225 g)
- package of vanilla sugar or 2 teaspoons vanilla extract
- 4 cups sifted confectioners' sugar or icing sugar (1 cup = 155 g)

- 1/2 teaspoon cream of tartar

Directions:

1. In a large mixing bowl beat the butter, vanillin, and cream of tartar with an electric mixer on medium speed until light and fluffy.
2. Add the confectioners' sugar, beating well. If necessary, gradually add 1/2 cup more confectioners' sugar. Scrape the bowl and beat again until the frosting is smooth and light.

Note: This frosting is also frequently made with a condensed-milk (sweetened) base, with the addition of flour to thicken the mixture.

Lemon frosting

Prep time: 10 minutes

Ingredients:

- Cream cheese
- Butter
- Vanilla extract
- Lemon juice
- Icing sugar.

Directions

1. Mix the cream cheese with the butter until it's creamy. Then mix in the vanilla extract and lemon juice. Gradually add icing sugar to make it less stiff and more spreadable.

Chocolate Glaze

Ingredients:

For the glaze:

- A cup (200 g) sugar
- pinch of salt, optional
- A cup (250 ml or 1/2 pint) water
- 9 ounces (255 g) unsweetened chocolate, chopped into small pieces
- 4 tablespoons unsalted butter
- teaspoon pure vanilla extract, or more to taste

Directions

1. Preheat oven to 350. Put the chocolate, butter, and sugar into a medium-sized bowl. Place over a pot of simmering water (make sure the bottom of the bowl doesn't touch the water). Stir constantly until melted and smooth. Remove from heat.
2. Mix in vanilla extract. Allow cooling to room temperature, stirring occasionally.
3. Pour glaze over cooled cake. Spread with a spatula or palette knife to coat evenly.
4. Allow sitting for at least an hour before serving. If you keep it in the refrigerator, the glaze will set faster.
5. You can also pour the glaze over individual pieces of cake to serve.

Conversion Chart

Volume Equivalents (Liquid)

US Standard	US Standard (Ounces)	Metric (Approximate)
2 tablespoons	1 fl. oz.	30 mL
¼ cup	2 fl. oz.	60 mL
½ cup	4 fl. oz.	120 mL
1 cup	8 fl. oz.	240 mL
1 and ½ cups	12 fl. oz.	355 mL
2 cups/1 pint	16 fl. oz.	475 mL
4 cups/ 1 quart	32 fl. oz.	1 L
1 gallon	128 fl. oz.	4 L

Volume Equivalents (Dry)

US Standard	Metric (Approximate)
1/8 teaspoon	0.5 mL
¼ teaspoon	1 mL
½ teaspoon	2 mL
¾ teaspoon	4 mL
1 teaspoon	5 mL
1 tablespoon	15 mL
¼ cup	59 mL
1/3 cup	79 mL
½ cup	118 mL
2/3 cup	156 mL
¾ cup	177 mL
1 cup	235 mL
2 cups	475 mL
3 cups	700 mL
4 cups	1 L

...nperatures

Fahrenheit (F)	Celsius (C) (Approximate)
250°	120°
300°	150°
325°	165°
350°	180°
375°	190°
400°	200°
425°	220°
450°	230°

Weight Equivalents

US Standard	Metric (Approximate)
½ ounce	15 g
1 ounce	30 g
2 ounces	60 g
4 ounces	115 g
8 ounces	225 g
12 ounces	340 g
16 ounces/1 pound	455 g

Conclusion

Baking for kids is about having fun, introducing good eating habits, and also enjoying treats in moderation. These recipes provide ideas for various baked foods, all are healthy and made from scratch, without adding preservatives or unnecessary extras.

Baking is a fun activity that brings joy to the person who bakes and helps prepare a snack for those around them. The warmth and delicious aroma of the preheated oven that comes from it while baking creates an atmosphere of comfort and convenience.

We, as adults, understand the importance of a healthy diet. Those who have learned that at a young age, what is a healthy diet, it is easier to stay healthy into adulthood.

Those who didn't necessarily have the healthiest diets growing up often struggle with their weight and health. At any point in life, people choose to eat healthily and get healthy, but surely from the start you want your children to eat healthily. A child can start helping you cook at a very young age as long as you advise them and hand them things to do that is within their skill level. It is also the best way to get them interested in healthy foods.

If you're learning to bake, you will find that working with the dough and mashing it is surely a great way to release some stress from a long school day or a long week. You might have some knowledge about cooking kitchen how-to, probably you've baked cookies before with your family or friends. Or probably you know nothing at all about cooking and that's alright as well because with this book you will learn how to become a pro in cooking.

In the kitchen, you have to practice to get better at it. Ensure that there is no need to get frustrated when things are not going as planned in a recipe because everyone can mess up while cooking. You just got to be patient and ask for help if you need it.

As a parent or adult, sometimes you are required to assist your child in baking. During the baking process, you are required to understand the dangers lurking when your child is baking that was not obvious to you. The list below is a compilation of the dangers and of ways to prevent your child from accidentally injuring others and themselves.

Ingredients

Firstly, do not leave your child without your knowledge to use any of the following Ingredients. Baking is not a science, but there is a certain degree of predictability that is required from the bakers, especially, young bakers.

. Glaze (honey, egg white)

. Baking powder

. Baking Soda

. Other Ingredients containing Baking Powder or Baking Soda

Preparation

Some Ingredients are highly flammable, such as oil. Therefore, ensure that your child removes any ingredient such as oil that may ignite or explode in a heated environment.

. Some are toxic if eaten in large doses, such as salt. Ensure that your child keeps safe the Ingredients at all times.

- Shredded coconut may be too difficult for young children to remove. Ensure that the child keeps his/her fingers protected when removing the coconut from the palm.

. Large grains are dangerous when inhaled. Ensure that your child does not inhale the Ingredients from the bowl.

. Certain Ingredients can be sharp to the touch. Close supervision may be required when your child is removing the Ingredients from the bowl.

. When your child is kneading the dough that may contain certain Ingredients, ensure that your child does not keep the chemicals in his/her mouth to see how it tastes.

. When handling some Ingredients, ensure that your child does not keep the ingredient in his/her bag or coat.

. Some Ingredients may make your child smell like a chemical. Ensure that your child does not wear his/her uniform as the scent may affect the class.

- Some Ingredients may stain your child's clothes. Ensure that your child is supervised at all times when handling food Ingredients.

. Some Ingredients may be hot when they are cooking. Ensure that your child knows how to handle medium and low heat when cooking.

Made in the USA
Coppell, TX
13 December 2022